M♥thers of B☺ys

SURVIVAL GUIDE

Funny adventures and tested advice on raising happy, independent boys

Written by Suzy Shaw, Mom
Illustrated by Beth Fisher

Copyright © 2024 Susan R. Sundius.

All rights reserved. No part of this book may be used or reproduced by any means, graphic, electronic, or mechanical, including photocopying, recording, taping or by any information storage retrieval system without the written permission of the author except in the case of brief quotations embodied in critical articles and reviews.

This book is a work of non-fiction. Unless otherwise noted, the author and the publisher make no explicit guarantees as to the accuracy of the information contained in this book and in some cases, names of people and places have been altered to protect their privacy.

Archway Publishing books may be ordered through booksellers or by contacting:

Archway Publishing
1663 Liberty Drive
Bloomington, IN 47403
www.archwaypublishing.com
844-669-3957

Because of the dynamic nature of the Internet, any web addresses or links contained in this book may have changed since publication and may no longer be valid. The views expressed in this work are solely those of the author and do not necessarily reflect the views of the publisher, and the publisher hereby disclaims any responsibility for them.

Interior Image Credit: Beth Fisher

ISBN: 978-1-6657-6311-0 (sc)
ISBN: 978-1-6657-6312-7 (e)

Library of Congress Control Number: 2024914508

Printed in China.

Archway Publishing rev. date: 11/22/2024

To the men in my life: Dan, my soulmate and life partner, and my boys, Jack and Will. Thank you for your encouragement and a life of adventures.

Acknowledgments

Don't let anyone tell you that writing a book is easy. This process has taken several years and a tribe of people. Please allow me to thank them now.

My husband Dan, a.k.a. Hon, and Jack, a.k.a. Earnest, read every variation of this book and encouraged me to keep going and fulfill my vision. Jack not only offered encouragement but pulled me back when I went too far and reminded me of stories that I had forgotten. When I asked Will, a.k.a. Exuberance, if he wanted me to delete or modify anything, he lovingly said, "It's your story, Mom. You tell it." I am so appreciative and proud of all three of them.

My parents gifted my brother and me with a loving home and a solid foundation. You don't realize how important that is when you're young. Looking back, it truly was a gift. You will discover nuggets of advice from my mother, Barby Shaw, throughout this book. I appreciate her sense of humor and know I got my funny bone from her. My brother Steve Shaw and his wife Susan always offered encouragement. Susan and my cousin Brad Fisher are also on a writing journey, and we often share information and advice. I truly appreciate having a supportive and encouraging family. I am also excited about sharing my adventures in parenting with the next generation of moms and my nieces, who are now raising boys of their own.

I have received inputs and suggestions from many members of my MOB (Mothers of Boys). Thank you, Cheryl Bohn, Joanne Byrne, Mary Ellen Connolly, Clare Crocker, Jerilyn Deitch, Katie Derr, Darlene Fierstein, Nichole Roberts, Sherry Sherwood, Andrea Snodgrass, and Monica Starr for reading the drafts and sharing your thoughts. Thank you too to the rest of the MOB for your friendship and for supporting me in sharing our stories.

Truth be told, I am a horrific speller, and this book only came to fruition with the help of Grammarly and a tribe of proofreaders. Thank you, Lori Jackman, Lyn McDermott, and Ann Sundius for being the comma police and appreciating the stories even though you do not have sons.

I also received professional help. Thank you, Amanda Ayers Barnett, editor with Kevin Anderson & Associates. Amanda has three boys of her own and offered valuable suggestions, comments, and encouragement. Erin Hagar provided the necessary support in landing the plane and wrapping this project up with comments, edits, organizational assistance, and coaching. I also appreciated the publishing advice from friends Dr. Paul Hokemeyer and Susan Hall, who shared their publishing experiences and lessons learned.

And finally, a shout-out to my incredibly creative team. Beth Fisher created illustrations out of photographs that I shared. She did not have the pleasure of growing up with a brother and was confused when I explained that I wanted them to look like "boy cartoons." My directions were "something between Calvin and Hobbes and The Family Circus." I think she nailed it! Her illustrations helped bring my vision together. I hope those shared life moments put a smile on your face. Thank you to Marnie Litz of Litz Art, who has also been instrumental in designing the book cover and branding for the MOB. And finally, a shout out to Pam Haskell of Chili Pepper Design, who is the best website designer in the business. Visit mothersofboys.life to see how it all comes together.

The Momma Journey

◀○▶

"Congratulations! You are a fully functioning human!" I texted my almost twenty-five-year-old son this message after he left the house following a weekend at the beach. He and his friend had pulled the sheets off the beds, put them and the dirty towels in the laundry basket, and picked up the room all before they left. These little acts without prodding would have been inconceivable a few years earlier. It was a completely relaxing weekend! The boys offered to pick up sandwiches on their way to the beach, remembered to grab a cooler, and paid for lunch with no expectation of hitting up the parent bank on the way to the deli. We all arrived *on time* at a predetermined location to drag our chairs, the cooler, and umbrellas across the sand and stake out our sunny spot. The whole weekend was lovely! No drama, just games, laughs, and minimal mess. Inconceivable!

After twenty-five years of reminding my two boys to put the dishes in the dishwasher, pick up the wet towels off the bathroom floor, and stop wrestling in the house, I was shocked when I realized that those conversations were no longer necessary. My husband and I gave each other a high five. We did it!

Raising kids is like a crazy roller-coaster ride. You chug slowly uphill, then your stomach flips as the ground drops out from under you, and you fly around the next corner. With each loop of the parenting roller coaster, your ability to anticipate what's next and to give a push when progress stalls, improves. Each child is different, and in some cases, you need to go back to the drawing board because what worked with one kid may not work with the next.

My husband and my goal was to raise our sons to be independent, happy, and well-rounded people. That meant letting the boys fail, allowing them to be empathetic, resilient, and succeed gracefully. It also means teaching them how to respect people and care for others.

It's been an interesting ride. With this book, I am sharing my lessons learned and my experiences in the hope that it will help you find your momma groove, have some (or a lot of) humor, and be a little kinder to yourself on the ups and downs of your roller-coaster story.

I have given just about everyone in this book a nickname because my cast of characters is not unique, and you will identify them in your life as well. Although the stories are mine, they are typical mother stories. I am sharing them because I believe our current culture of social media and keeping up with the Joneses and Kardashians have created unrealistic expectations of how to be a functioning mother. So here is my story of love, chaos, and growth so that you may laugh and think, "I've got this!"

The Beginning

I met my husband in my early thirties and got married at thirty-two. He is the seventh of nine kids and has three brothers and five sisters. One of his sisters was my roommate, which is how we met. At that time, we were living in Baltimore, earning my husband a Baltimore nickname of "Hon," short for honey. Our boys have twenty-five first cousins, now ranging in age from forty-five to fourteen. We have a very large tribe!

My husband, "Hon," and I had our first son just before I turned thirty-five and the second just before I turned thirty-seven. The boys are twenty-one months apart. One weekend, Hon's sister and family graciously offered to watch the boys so that we could go to a party out of town. When we picked up the boys after a night away, Hon's sister proclaimed that she had renamed them Earnest and Exuberance. Earnest, the firstborn, to this day, is still quieter, intuitive, and loves to laugh. Exuberance, also called "Me Too," is certain he can do *everything* his older brother can do while leaping tall buildings wearing a cape. My baby factory closed after Exuberance because I was determined not to have more children than I had hands.

I do not think of myself as someone born to be a mom. My mom is that person. She was a kindergarten teacher, full of funny songs and true knowledge of how kids operate. Me? I'm a realist who learns from my mistakes, adapts, and appreciates the wins. I didn't feel as if I was born to be a mother. I stumbled through my on-the-job momma training. But looking back, I have very few regrets, and most of my regrets were that I was harder on myself than I needed to be. Slowing down and thinking before I acted became a key to success.

I didn't pause my career after the short people arrived and always struggled to balance my career and home life. My career began in TV production, and I have ridden the communication wave during my career and adapted to the seismic shifts in my profession and technology. I held on tight as video became high definition, the Internet was born, the IoT (Internet of Things) sprang into our hands in the form of a cell phone, and our appliances started talking to us. The world seemed to move at a much quicker pace than it did when I was a kid.

Days before I delivered Exuberance, the Columbine High School massacre occurred. I was essentially bedridden during that time and in a lot of pain due to the baby pushing on my sciatic nerve. I spent those days watching the news in horror and overwhelmed by the societal changes that my children were going to grow up in. Sandy Hook, 9-11, Virginia Tech, George Floyd, Me Too, COVID-19, January 6, and more changed our society so that now traumas seem commonplace. These concerns are part of the parenting fabric, and having frank conversations with my boys as they grew up helped us address the unknowns in the future.

This book is framed around boys since that is my experience. It may be relevant for the girls in your house as well. Each child is different, and as moms, we must grab little pieces of knowledge where we can and stitch them into a new parenting playbook. Because I am interested in a wide range of topics around raising children, I have launched a companion podcast to this book, also called *Mothers of Boys Survival Guide*. The podcast invites experts to discuss topics and share practical advice with parents. The podcasts are relatively short and created as quick tips you can listen to as you jump in the car to transport your tribe or walk around the block with the dog.

The Basics

As I look back, I realize there were several themes that I emphasized to my boys since they were little. The one that got the most airplay is "I am not raising dumb boys. I expect you to think for yourself!" You might presume that telling your child to think before acting would not be something you needed to say repeatedly, but the blank stares that came back at me during these moments convinced me that I couldn't say it too often. By the time they became teenagers, this mantra became "Think. Just *think*." This did not come easily to my boys, but they finally got it down and are now rocking it!

Another ongoing theme was that *fair* and *even* were unrealistic expectations. I recognized that my parenting style was going to be different for each kid, so I rarely felt the need to be equitable. If I did something for one kid, I did not feel I had to do the same for the other. Hon initially struggled with my cavalier attitude about parenting equality. He grew up with eight siblings, and as the seventh of nine, his parents had well-defined parenting management and expectations for the four boys and five girls by the time he was toddling around. I imagine that equality was a manner of survival in a large family. For us, with only two children, acknowledging early on this *inequality* with the boys paid off throughout their lives. It began with Christmas, not feeling the need to calculate toy equality, then moved on to a thousand other things—sports, school supplies, trips, a car, school loans, and overall financial support. They are different humans; they need different things, and in my opinion, equality of support is not realistic.

The attitude that got me through the parenting journey was to remember my sense of humor. There are so many moments that as a mother of boys, I would start cracking myself up. For example, teaching a little boy to pee in the toilet. It's just hysterical. I didn't know how to pee standing up, *but* I was very vested in them learning how to do it correctly and clean up after themselves if their aim was poor. Sure, Hon helped with the fundamentals, but the day-to-day reminders landed squarely on me and the women who provided daycare.

The MOB

I could not have survived without my Mothers of Boys friends, a.k.a. the MOB. Knowing other mothers of boys is critical to your sanity. When your kids are little, the MOB will be the people you turn to when you need an adult conversation, a playmate, and a daycare backup plan. When the boys became older, the MOB was on the lookout, running surveillance when you were not around, and the group you turned to and shared your child's heartaches and successes. I had, and still have, several MOB groups. The friends that earned the nickname of "the MOB" were Exuberance's friends' moms. That pack of boys was *busy*, and it took all of us to keep up with them. You'll hear more about that later.

The beautiful thing about the members of the MOB is that we were all very different. We understood and worried about different things while sharing our concerns, heartbreaks, and triumphs. We supported and carried each other through sickness and tragedy. In this culture of social media's imagined perfection, the honesty of the MOB was powerful. I strongly suggest you nurture your MOB. The advice and support are invaluable.

Members of the MOB had different strengths. I was the tech mom and kept track of the boys on social media and shared tips for monitoring activities. There were a few safety moms who alerted the rest of us when we were clueless. There were road trip moms who would scoop up the pack and take them to look for fossils in the mud, go for a hike, or go to the beach or a ski slope. Bless them for there is nothing better than a tired boy!

Some of the moms had daughters. This was incredibly helpful because you can miss a lot of pop culture and trends when you only have boys. For example, we made some new friends in our neighborhood, and they invited Hon and me out to a Happy Hour. Our friends texted their excitement that their "new BFFs could meet them sans offspring." Hon and I had no idea what a BFF was! BFF was a new abbreviation for us. Our boys didn't call anyone a BFF. We took a guess and decided it stood for "Best F— in' Friend." When we told our new friends what we had guessed BFF stood for, they howled. "Best Friends Forever" was not a possibility we had considered. We still laugh that we put the F in BFF. The MOB will set you straight, point out the errors in your assumptions, and be your BFFs forever.

By reading this book, you are now an official member of my MOB. It is my hope that you get a chuckle and some tips and are a little kinder to yourself when you have similar experiences with your boys. I wish you well in your parenting journey!

The Golden Goo

Being a mom means becoming the chief manufacturer at the golden goo[1] factory. It's difficult to explain a mother's love for her family, her children, and her children's friends and family. I call it *golden goo*, the fuel that makes the family run. It's the heart that makes the house a home.

---

[1] Golden goo: Some women ooze love. I called it golden goo, and little and big kids flock to them like honey.

There is not an endless supply of golden goo. There will be times when you have enough for a whole classroom of runny-nosed kids, and other times when you are so tired that you barely have a cup to spare. As I got the hang of being a mother, I was better able to take care of myself and had more of the precious supply to share. Golden goo is invaluable, better than money or toys. Some women have it in spades! And kids zip off to them like bees to honey.

Me? I was exhausted, juggling a husband, a job, and young kids. Appreciating how to balance yourself and the needs of your career and family is difficult. That's why your support systems—family, babysitters, and the incredible MOB—are critical to your sanity.

Being a parent is a marathon, not a sprint. When my kids were young, I was in survival mode and had trouble finding time for myself. Hon was traveling for his job and earning his master's degree. I had my own company and career and felt like I was the ringmaster in a three-ring circus. Life balance is something I had to work for. Keep in mind that balance comes and goes like waves. One minute, you have it, then the next, you don't. As your kids become more independent, other elements of your life can become more complicated. I strongly suggest that you find ways to make time for the things that fill you up: reading, exercising, playing music, or walking in a park. Whatever it is, taking time for *your* needs are part of the equation to keep the golden goo flowing. When I eventually got my footing and humor back, that golden goo was all around.

As your kids grow, remember that even that boy in the large body with the immature brain looking down on you because you are now shorter, needs golden goo. He needs a hug. He needs the mama ear that listens to all his troubles and offers some simple advice. The golden goo keeps them coming back home even as adults.

Men are capable of golden goo too. Although it seems to be less obvious, I know men who are the Pied Piper of children.

Even babies, feeling safe and warm, quiet down and snuggle in. Encourage those moments with your husband when you see them happening and take advantage of that time to replenish your golden goo.

How the Book Is Organized

I have done my best to keep the book in chronological order of both the boys' growth and mine as a mother. Some topics are cyclical and mature as the boys evolve.

The graph on the next page depicts our journey. The Y axis is the quest for independence, and the X axis is the age of the boys. For the sake of this illustration, the line is straight, but I guarantee it was quite wiggly. The top of the line shows the growth of the boys with the nicknames I gave for those milestones. In the beginning, it seemed like they had a death wish, and I was on high alert. The *death wish stage* declined at about age three when they began to follow simple instructions, and Band-Aids were replaced by balls, many balls of all kinds. I called puberty the *man-cub stage*. Suddenly, my little boys were looking down at me, and they bounced off doorframes as they became familiar with their new larger size. It was during this stage that I recognized that my parenting style needed to adapt quickly. Since I had no desire to become a helicopter parent, I referred to myself as a *submarine parent*. I floated beneath the surface, pinging locations, confirming data, and monitoring activities, and on occasion, I had a full breach and emerged on the surface to bring the craziness back into compliance. The final stage of my graph shows their *remarkable transformation*. This occurred in their early twenties. Just when I thought I'd be picking wet towels off the floor forever, *bam*, they got it. And it was truly remarkable. My parenting style changed during this phase, too. Now as empty nesters, Hon and I adapted. I admit it's a bit weird, beginning to prioritize your own needs again after decades of child-rearing.

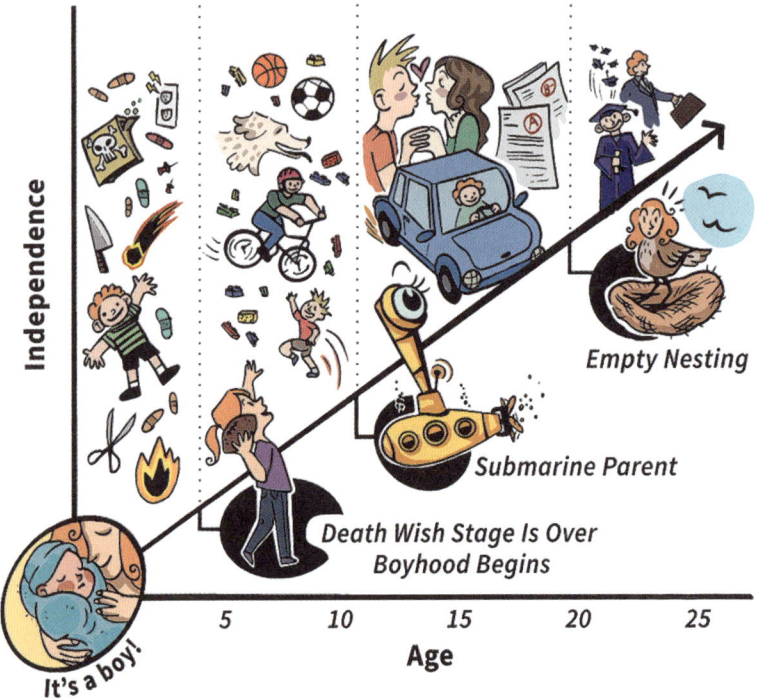

Since I appreciate that moms don't have much time to read, the stories are typically short, so you can feel accomplished after reading one and passing out from exhaustion. There are also random sidebars: "Tips" from me and "Sister Sense," which are tips I picked up from my nine sisters-in-law and sister-friends, who are way too many to count. I hope that by the end of this book, you know that you are part of the MOB, that you appreciate the laughs, and that you stay kind to yourself on this parenting journey.

Tabe of Contents

The Momma Journey 4

Surviving the Early Years: Babies and Toddlers 14

Elementary School 58

Middle School 87

High School 124

The Remarkable Transformation 158

About the Author 179

Surviving the Early Years: Babies and Toddlers

◄◦►

When my kids become wild and unruly, I use a nice, safe playpen. When they're finished, I climb out.
—Erma Bombeck

Nature versus Nurture

Before I had children, I had this notion that good parenting could fix almost anything and that *nurture* was the key. I didn't appreciate how unique each person was until I had children. When you put the DNA of both parents into the wheel of fortune and give it a spin, you really do not know what's going to emerge. Siblings who you would think should be similar due to the same parents and environment still can be as different as night and day.

You try to use the same parenting playbook with all your kids, but in my experience, it will come out 180 degrees different. I tell friends with only one child that the reason to have two or more children is so you know when something goes awry that it's them (nature) and not you (nurture). Yes, I sort of mean that as a joke, but when you have more than one child, it becomes much more obvious that your ability to control another person is not possible and that nurture is really about a million little touchpoints to keep your little person on a path forward. A strategy that works with one child can be a complete failure with another. Stay nimble, my friends! Nature is a talented adversary.

Keep It Simple: Basic Survival Tips with an Infant

Newborns offer us the chance to get our footing as mothers before our children kick into high gear. The early days are about learning the importance of balance, tone, and tribe.

Balance is understanding how important it is to sleep when the baby sleeps. I was so tired with Earnest that my milk did not flow very well. As a new mother, I did not have or genuinely understand balance. The reality was that I couldn't do it *all* anymore and had to be realistic about what I could accomplish. With the arrival of baby two, Exuberance, my ability to balance my life became harder. My recommendation is to lower the bar for what you are able to accomplish, especially when they are under three years old. Earnest went to a home daycare a few days a week after Exuberance was born, so I could try to recover from childbirth and the other obligations of life.

To be honest, I didn't learn balance until I had my second baby and was really forced to ask for more help with everything: cooking, cleaning, business, and childcare. I was beyond exhausted during my second pregnancy. Also, the baby was pushing against my sciatic nerve, making it difficult to walk. Earnest was a toddler and recognized that it was difficult for me to catch him. He would take off running when I got him out of the car. I could not carry him at that point due to the pregnancy and recognized it was a bad look to drag your toddler by the arm up the stairs of your house. That forced me to reach out to my neighbors for help. I would call them on my way into the neighborhood, and one of them would meet me in the driveway to help herd Earnest into the house. Those neighbors, Rose and Kerry, became a lifeline to our family and adopted grandparents to the boys. In my mind's eye, I can still see Earnest dashing across the lawn to Kerry working in the yard, shouting, "What doing, Kerry?" Of course, Kerry always needed help and welcomed spending time with Earnest.

> **Tip: Lower the Bar**
>
> I was a small business owner, so I had no maternity leave. For me, maternity leave was business debt, and I had to be realistic and prioritize what I could accomplish and lower the bar of being all things to all people.
>
> The simple fact is that children change your life, and for me, I had to be picky about what work I accepted. The trick to lowering the bar is to simplify and be realistic about what additional responsibilities you can commit to.

Tone refers to finding your calm strength and ways to be still with your baby. It is critical to bond with your newborn in the first few months of their life, so they can feel your warmth and safety. One of my favorite examples of tone was singing songs and lullabies. The *House at Pooh Corner* by Loggins and Messina was my go-to when putting the babies to bed and was part of our nighttime routine.

To have balance and a positive tone, you need a tribe! A spouse, significant other, family, sitters, and the MOB are critical to keeping your sanity and well-being. When Earnest was a newborn, he was colicky. It was a guessing game as to why he was crying and fussing. I remember driving to see family just to give myself a break from trying to comfort him.

Parenting styles and expectations have changed over the generations. I grew up in a time when mom was in charge of the kids and the house, and dad was responsible for finances. I have very few memories of my dad participating in my after-school activities, like Girl Scouts, softball, and guitar lessons. My dad's participation was not expected. Hon and I had different goals for coparenting, where he would take a much more active role than in the homes we grew up in.

The Four S: Sleep, Sanity, Sustenance, and Safety

Sleep

Coparenting began immediately with late-night feeding and efforts to get cranky, colicky Earnest back to sleep. Hon would bounce and bounce him to try to get him to burp and go back to sleep. If you heard Hon talk, you'd understand that singing is not in his wheelhouse, so his nighttime lullaby was to recite the Pledge of Allegiance. Sometimes Hon would just pass out with the baby in the recliner. Your sleep is as critical as getting your child to sleep. Recovery from childbirth and getting your footing with an infant is not easy. Ask your partner and family for help and prioritize your sleep and your baby's equally.

As a new mom, figuring out how to get my baby to go to sleep was nerve-racking. Earnest did not like being put down and cried when he was put into his crib. Three months in, I was exhausted, and Hon was heading overseas for two weeks of work. I moved in with my parents to get help and talked with our pediatrician, Dr. B., about how to get Earnest to go to bed without being held and rocked. Earnest was a healthy and strong three-month-old baby. Dr. B. said he was old enough to learn how to comfort himself and go to sleep without being held. With encouragement from my mom and Dr. B., I put Earnest to bed and shut the door. It took thirty minutes that first night for Earnest to stop fussing and fall asleep. The next night, it took twenty-five minutes; and the time continued to decline until, by the time Hon returned, Earnest was in the groove and barely crying when he was laid down in his crib for bed. You will hear many opinions of how to get a baby to fall asleep, and what worked for Earnest typically didn't work for Exuberance. The only thing I can promise is this stage will end with patience and a routine.

> ### Sister Sense—Blankets
>
> Having blankets stashed in high-probability nap locations like a car seat is critical. Blankies tend to disappear. Don't be caught unprepared and stash them for emergency use!
>
> Exuberance's greatest love was his blanket. Actually, any blanket would do! At one point, he discovered the mother lode of blankies, the drawer of kitchen towels, and it was impossible to keep them in plain sight. Luckily, the kitchen towel stage was short-lived.

Sleep, Don't Underestimate Its Power

My career as a video producer gave me a wonderful opportunity to interview amazing people and visit unique places. Once, I spent a week recording footage at an insomnia clinic. I interviewed psychologists, cardiologists, technicians, and several patients. The sleep psychologist explained that most people have insomnia because of poor *sleep hygiene*. Sleep hygiene refers to the rituals around going to sleep. It's both environmental and physical. Poor environmental conditions may include going to bed with the TV on with its flickering light and sound, working on a laptop, or playing with your cell phone, and then expecting to roll over and fall asleep. Physical conditions might include not exercising during the day or drinking caffeine or a sugary drink just before bedtime.

The doctor recommended being aware of your bedtime habits. With our boys, we developed a bedtime routine where they had a bath after dinner and got to play in the tub, then pajamas, a book and bed.

Now, I'm not standing on high and proclaiming the house shall be silent when trying to get the kiddos to sleep! Quick buy blackout curtains! Juggling kids of multiple ages' sleeping schedules can make you crazy, and good grief, they need to learn to adapt and roll with family dynamics. Earnest always had difficulty falling asleep, but he knew better than to get out of his crib. He would talk to his stuffed animals and sing himself to sleep.

Exuberance loved sleeping but would go down in a final burst of energy we called the *last burn*.[2] He was like a rocket ship lighting off the last bit of fuel before heading into space. You could

> **Tips for Sleeping In**
>
> I have no tips for getting an infant to sleep in. Good luck with that! When my brother and I were toddlers, my mom would leave a small cereal box of Cheerios in my crib and explain that I had to eat them one at a time. She would get an extra thirty minutes on the challenge of opening the box alone. That tip worked for my kids too.
>
> When Earnest was big enough to get up on his own and Exuberance was still in a crib, we used to leave a juice and yogurt on the bottom shelf of the refrigerator and the TV set to PBS. He would happily have chill time before Exuberance turned up the energy.

---

[2] The last burn: The moments of exuberance and energy just before bed, like burning off the last bit of fuel.

tell bedtime was coming because he'd get silly, spinning and flailing until he threw himself down on the floor into a tired cry. The last burn was the giveaway to scoop him up and toss him in bed for the night.

When the boys woke us up in the middle of the night about a nightmare, we would make a big deal of it in a positive way: "Wow! You must have really been sound asleep for your body to have to make up a scary dream to wake you up to go to the bathroom! That's the body's last resort to keep you from wetting the bed!" Then we'd shuffle them to the bathroom and back into their bed. There came the point when they didn't wake us up to tell us about the nightmare, and they just used the bathroom and went back to bed.

My motto then was, "The more they sleep, the more they sleep; the less they sleep, the less they sleep." That meant that if I woke them up to try to get on a schedule that worked for me, the day would be a disaster. They would be cranky, and it would throw their whole sleeping schedule off. If I put them to bed on our typical schedule and let them wake up on their own, they slept as much as they needed to and were happy. (And so were we!)

A tip we learned from friends whose kids happily went off to bed was to get your toddler attached to a stuffed animal or blanket and make sure it never left their bed. Earnest had a stuffed pig from the book *If You Give a Pig a Pancake*. He wanted Piggy to be with him at all times, so I had to get tricky and distract him so that Piggy could be returned to the crib. When naptime came around, I'd say, "Don't you want to tell Piggy about your day?" And off he went to bed.

Sanity: Sharing the Load

One of my early parenting lessons was accepting that someone else would help care for my infant and do it differently. It reminded me of a conversation I had with my aunt one year after Thanksgiving dinner. She was complaining to my uncle about how he was cleaning the dishes. I asked her why she was complaining. "Do you want to wash the dishes?"

"He is ruining my pots and pans using a steel wool pad," she said.

I asked, "Why don't you hide the steel wool pads? If you don't want to do it yourself, I suggest not complaining about how it's being done."

She laughed, smiled, thanked me, and then thanked my uncle for doing the dishes.

I remember having the same conversation in my head the first time I saw Hon microwaving a plastic bottle for our newborn. I gently explained why it's not a good idea to microwave plastic. Then shared the recommended method and let him continue. Sharing the load with family, friends, and caregivers is essential for allowing the new mom to recover from childbirth and find her balance.

Sister Sense—Teething

Freeze plain mini bagels or cut up full-sized bagels into quarters. Teething gums hurt, but teething rings can be too cold to hold. A frozen mini bagel in a highchair means you can almost finish making dinner! They love the cold and appreciate the taste of food. Keep an eye on it as it defrosts, for toward the end, it turns into a mess and a possible choking hazard.

Sanity (Yours and Theirs)

"Never argue, distract instead." This is one of my mother's best recommendations, and she might have adapted it from Mark Twain's saying, "Never argue with a fool, onlookers may not be able to tell the difference." There is nothing like trying to rationalize with a little person, especially when they are tired or hungry.

What works is to hear them out, repeat it back to them with your answer (often no), and before they can speak again, point out something irrelevant to the conversation. "No, we can't go to the park right now. Look at that cloud! It looks like a dinosaur!"

Earnest broke me in on my veiled hope of sanity when he taught me about time, which was a regular topic when discussing the possibility of an outing.

Earnest, "Can we go to the zoo?"

"We're going to go tomorrow."

Blank stare. Earnest understood two time periods: now and to-later. "To-later" was any time that was not now. Next week, tomorrow, Thursday meant nothing to him.

"Are we going to go to-later?"

"Yes. We are going to the zoo to-later. Would you like to go to the park?"

Earnest's Great Adventure—A little brother!

I delivered Exuberance just before I turned thirty-seven. As I was nearing his delivery date, a good friend who was a pediatrician gave us some little gifts for Earnest. She said the older sibling sometimes feels left out when the new baby arrives. To help him feel special, give him these little presents when he comes to the hospital to see his new brother. It was a great tip, and Earnest was proud to be a big brother.

Of course, my water broke with Exuberance in the middle

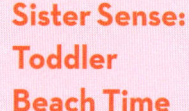

Sister Sense: Toddler Beach Time

A five dollar blow up pool + two buckets of water + sand crab = toddler entertainment all day!

Set up the little blow-up pool under an umbrella with a little bit of water, a sand crab or two, and some plastic cups for happy toddler time.

of the night. Our plan to have our neighbors, Rose and Kerry, watch Earnest failed when we couldn't wake them up. So Earnest was scooped up to go get his new brother from the hospital.

Earnest did not appreciate being part of the middle-of-the-night new baby brother pickup team. Of course, Hon's car was low on gas, so the first stop was to fill up the tank. Earnest was sobbing in his car seat in the back seat. I turned to him and said, "Hey, we're going on an adventure. Don't you want to go on an adventure?"

The crying paused. Earnest's favorite movie at that time was *Barney's Great Adventure*. "An adventure?" he asked.

"Yes, to get your new baby brother," I explained. Well now, this was a horse of a different color, and he perked right up.

Hon jumped back into the car, and Earnest exclaimed, "Daddy, we're going on an adventure! We're going to get my new baby brother!" Hon looked at me with relief that he didn't have to listen to crying all the way to the hospital.

Thankfully, my mom met us at the hospital in the middle of the night and retrieved Earnest. After the delivery, she brought him back to meet his new little brother, and he proudly put on a T-shirt from the hospital store that said, "I'm a big brother," and gently held Exuberance with help from Hon.

Earnest quickly became the *go-to* kid as he ran to pick up dropped items. He valued his importance in the new family dynamic, and his favorite thing to do was to stick the pacifier back in Exuberance's mouth if he was crying. It was also a lot of fun to pull it out and hear the sucking pop come out of his little brother.

Earnest teaches his new baby brother to tolerate things taken away from him.

Travel Essentials

When Earnest was a toddler, I got him a little dinosaur sleeping bag. Most of the time, it was in his crib or toddler bed, but if we traveled, the sleeping bag came with us on the road. We could put that dinosaur sleeping bag down wherever he went to bed, tuck in his beloved stuffed Piggy and his blanket, and he felt at home. Exuberance's sleeping bag was a race car because he fell asleep fast!

As the boys grew older and started to push back on naps, I used the sleeping bags to get a break and get something done. "Go get your sleeping bags, and you can watch a movie instead of a nap!" We'd put the bags down on the rug, and I'd put on a movie with the sound nearly at an inaudible level, so they wouldn't hear the TV if they moved or wrestled. Exuberance always fell asleep, and Earnest and I got a break. *Holes* was one of my favorite movies to play. The characters dug a lot of holes, which is an excellent time to nod off.

Side Note: I always tried to keep *the force*[3], a.k.a. the television remote control, up high on a piece of furniture so that only Hon and I could reach it to turn it on and change the channel or volume. I called it the force because whoever had it had the power!

Sustenance: Be Kind to Yourself!

This journey of parenting has its ups and downs. It's critical to take care of *and* be kind to yourself. I was my biggest critic, which truly is not helpful.

For example, I remember feeling such pressure to breastfeed successfully. I was so exhausted with my first

> **Be Kind to Yourself**
>
> Please be kind to yourself on this journey of motherhood. I think many women are their own worst critics. Don't fall into that rut. Raising quality humans is the hardest job on earth and don't let anyone tell you differently.

---

[3] The force: The nickname for the television remote control because whoever has the remote has the force.

pregnancy that my milk didn't flow well, and it seemed that Earnest was always hungry. Two weeks after Exuberance's birth, I found a deer tick bullseye on my stomach. I think it hitchhiked in on the cat because I wasn't exactly frolicking in the woods at that time. I started a twenty-one-day antibiotic treatment to ward off the possibility of Lyme disease.

The doctor told me that "all studies show that Lyme disease does not pass through breast milk."

"Who signs up for that study?" I asked the doctor.

Blank stare from the doctor. Logic trips them up every time.

I did choose to stop breastfeeding after starting the antibiotics. This choice initially made me a bit frustrated since my milk was flowing much better than with Earnest. After enduring the pain of my breast milk drying up, the switch to a bottle was easy. The bonus was that there was more help available for feeding. Even big brother Earnest was willing to hold the bottle for Exuberance!

The Three-Legged Stool Philosophy

When you become a parent, you build systems to manage the chaos. Thus, when the kids were little, I made up the three-legged stool philosophy of males.

My aunt has an antique three-legged birthing stool, which has always fascinated me. I found it amazing that this three-legged piece of furniture could be sturdy enough to deliver a baby. Apparently, three legs of support are all you need.

I believe that 90 percent of the issues can be fixed with these three things:

Antique birthing stool

1. Food–Let's face it, the critters fall apart when they're hungry (and thirsty)!
2. Exercise–Just like a dog, you need to run them every day!
3. Sleep–They need at least eight hours of sleep, or they are cranky.

In practice, the philosophy sounds like this:

Your son melts down—"Can I get you something to eat?"

Your son eats and continues to melt down—"Let's see how fast you can run around the house. Ready, set, go!"

Your son comes back in and is still unbearable—"Go to bed!"

This system works almost right from the beginning although when they're babies, you need to check diapers too.

Safety and Surviving the "Death Wish Stage"

Thank goodness my babies came out of the womb not moving very much! It gave us time to figure out the basic bodily functions of eating, pooping, and sleeping before they were mobile. Once toddlers discover they can go places, that's all they want to do.

Somewhere around six to nine months, my boys entered the *death-wish stage*,[4] which seemed to last until three years of age. First, they realized that they could move under their own power. Then they realize they can run away from *you*! It's quite shocking how fast those little feet can go. A mom with boys is like the queen of the meerkats with her ears pressed back, listening for danger, eyes scanning the environment for threats, and for good reason because her child has a death wish!

Even Earnest was quite capable of throwing himself into the fireplace hearth during this stage. His first word was *hot*. His second word was *hot dog*. It says a lot about his concern over being burned and his limited diet. I wish I could tell you what Exuberance's first word was, but I was too tired and was then chasing two little people to remember that kind of milestone.

The death-wish stage was a critical time in my boy's development. It seems pain is an important element to their learning process, not just once, but multiple times to prove to themselves that "Yes, running into the table is something that should be avoided." Now granted, their bodies are top-heavy. That big head of theirs makes them off-kilter. When combined with the gait of a drunken sailor, falling is inevitable. When

---

[4] Death-wish stage: The period between ages one and three when little people have no concept of danger and live with abandon. This stage returns for a period when they are teenagers.

you have more than one boy, it's not only inevitable, it's a game. The boys were always challenging each other with tripping, pushing, and shoving, then *boom*! They learn critical life skills during this stage: how to get back up, stick up for themselves, not harm others, sound the alarm, and run for Mom's golden goo if things get too bad.

Before Exuberance was born, Earnest shared a babysitter a few days a week with his cousin, Ry, who was five weeks younger. One day after picking Earnest up, I noticed he had bruises and scratches on his chunky ankles. The next time I dropped him off, Earnest wiggled out of my arms to go play with Ry, then snagged the toy that Ry was playing with and took off. Ry had not learned to walk yet, but he could commando crawl faster than any child I've ever seen. He caught Earnest by the leg and bit him on the calf. I suddenly understood the cause of the bruises and scratches. This was typical boy play during the death-wish stage. They will laugh, cry, hit, bite, hug, and run, all within thirty seconds. It was important to help them understand that physically hurting another person was not acceptable. Since an action (taking a

> **Safety First Tips**
>
> - Make use of gates, barriers, and be sure to pad sharp corners.
>
> - We added a gate to our deck, which turned it into a giant play pen.
>
> - They are short! Get on your knees, crawl around and look for danger.
>
> - Put all your plastic kitchen storage containers in one lower cabinet that they can play in while you are cooking.
>
> - They are on a mission to understand boundaries. Give them space.
>
> - Move sentimental objects out of reach and a few non-breakable irresistible items lower so you may teach little hands how to "look" without breaking.

toy and running) initiated a reaction (a bite), it was important to try to explain cause and effect. They did not get it initially, but it's a critical life lesson and worth repeating over and over again.

My boys' go-to response to frustration was often physical. They'd cry, throw themselves on the floor, spin around like the Tasmanian devil, and stomp their feet. These acts were often impressive and done in the most public of spaces for greater effect. Once, Exuberance had one of these meltdowns in the middle of the grocery store. He wanted something. I was not paying attention and just said, "No," so he threw himself onto the floor, flailing about with flair and volume. Then he had my attention, and it was time to talk.

I asked him what he was doing, and he made his demand. I repeated with calm opposition, my no answer. The tantrum continued. I finally leaned over him flailing on the floor and said, "Is this working for you? Are you getting what you want? If it's working for you, then by all means, I think you should keep it up. If it's not, you might want to consider acting differently." And then I waited.

He slammed his hands on the ground. "It's not working!"

"That's what I thought too," I said. He got off the floor and I scooped him up, plopped him in the shopping cart, and we wrapped up grocery shopping.

As a rule, I tried not to feed negative energy with more bad energy, a.k.a. anger. In my experience, temper tantrums typically pass quickly, and it is easier to rationalize with a calm child than one having a temper tantrum. I am also quite certain that following the trip to the store was a snack, a run around the house, and a nap, thus applying the three-legged stool philosophy.

Sick Kids

Yes, you have an incredible germ factory living in your house. These little bundles of love build up their immunity the hard way by getting sick. We were blessed to have Dr. B. as our pediatrician and could call the office to get help in determining if we should bring the boys in for a sick visit. Hon and I experienced kids with runny noses, viruses, ear infections, croup, strep throat, and an emergency trip to the hospital for a febrile seizure, all before enrollment in elementary school. These sudden illnesses require coordination of the person with the *give job* or a backup like a grandparent.

Because both Hon and I had jobs, we had to figure out how to juggle raising kids with our careers. Usually, my job was the give job in that if something happened, like a sick kid, my job would be flexible, and I'd stay home. I recommend having the "who has the give job" conversation with your significant other ahead of time and reaching a joint decision before the need arises. There is a great reduction in parenting stress if you identify several options for addressing a "little man down" scenario.

> **Tip: The Give Job**
>
> When there are two working parents it's important to discuss flexibility. How will your family adapt to sudden schedule disruptions? Whose schedule can adapt to meet the need of the moment. The need for a plan is critical and inevitable. Identifying who will have the give job ahead of time will reduce parenting stress and conflicts. In our case, the give job was primarily mine, but there were times Hon had to make adjustments. This was not a one and done discussion, and we had to tag team until they were independent.

So what did I learn? (This is *my* experience. Please consult your favorite doctor first!)

- Teething—It hurts! A frozen washcloth, frozen mini-bagel, popsicle, teething gel, and baby pain relievers are essential.
- Croup—Croup, which sounds like a seal barking, drags you out of bed in a panic in the middle of the night. Dr. B.'s best tip to us was to wrap the boys up in a blanket and take them

outside to breathe in the night air. The cold air is like an ice pack to the inflamed lungs, and it's easier than sticking their head in the freezer or a steam shower. Hon would sit on our deck with Earnest, asking him to breathe deep and look at the stars. With the cold night air, his coughing would subside, and he'd settle all snug with his dad. After ten minutes, he'd be ready to go back to bed.

- Bugs–There were *so* many viruses that they were often throwing up or had diarrhea. I would get them to lie on their left side on the couch with a bucket in case they were sick while watching television. Lying on the left side is almost a miracle for nausea, as it allows gases to escape and the person to feel less nauseous.
- Tubby toast–*Teletubbies* was a popular kid's show at that time, so when they were sick with a virus and on the BRAT (bananas, rice, applesauce, and toast) diet, the tubby toast was the ticket. It's simple: a piece of bread with butter, sugar, and cinnamon that is broiled, so the sugar caramelizes on the top.
- Growing pains are real!–Exuberance would wake up crying in the night that his shins and ankles hurt. *Why* is it always in the *middle of the night?* A little massage and pain reliever helped us all get back to bed.
- Keep them home–As much as you want to send those snotty-nosed, whiney boys off to daycare and school, try to refrain and keep them home. They will recover quicker, and the teachers, caregivers, and other parents will appreciate your thoughtfulness.
- Patience–It is key to your sanity and your child's healing. This too will pass!

Little Kids, Little Problems

There's a saying among parents that percolates to the surface at some point near middle/high school, "Little kids, little problems."

Big kids, big problems." I wish I understood this perspective when my kids were little. When you look back, you realize all the building blocks that you, your partner, family, daycare providers, and teachers laid down during the preschool and elementary school time frame. In this section, I share some of my lessons learned, funny stories, and parenting tips. Please understand that my strategies may not be the right fit for your family, and I'm just providing food for thought.

NO Is a Great Word

All people want to be heard, and little kids are no different. Sifting through endless requests is a big part of parenting. I had the greatest success when I first listened and then repeated the request, proving that I heard and understood it. Then there were only three possible answers: "yes," "no," and "I'll think about it." I rarely said, "I'll think about it," when the boys were little, but as they grew older and the request got more complicated, "I'll think about it" allowed me to get input from Hon and the MOB. Once I had time to think about it, then the answer was yes or no.

My boys did not do well with gray answers like "maybe." A gray answer was an opportunity for renegotiation and the challenge to wear me down. I learned to be a "yes or no" mom. When you volunteer in school, you can spot the kids who do not understand the meaning of no. Utilizing a simple yes or no strategy paid me back in spades when the boys hit puberty, but the training starts before they can even talk. To a toddler, no means hot or game on. They either stop dead in their tracks or take off like a squirrel with a nut. Saying no with a calm but stern voice is the key to your little man not running away. I never found yelling a productive communication style, and if you don't sound firm enough, even little kids will not take you seriously. It is only through repeated, calm yes or no training, that no means no sinks in. Don't delay getting started on this training, as I found it to be a critical technique in my survival.

Self-Entertainable

When the boys were little, self-entertainment could also mean trouble! There was no end to what they could get into. To keep them busy, I would give them a job. Here are some of my favorite toddler/preschool jobs:

Painting–I would grab an old paintbrush and a plastic cup of water and ask the boys to paint the deck or the sidewalk. The water turns the surface darker, making the kids think they are really painting. I used this trick outside to answer a quick email, make a call, weed the garden, or do other multitasking mom stuff.

The boys "paint" the deck with water.

Crafts–Making playdough is really easy, is nontoxic, and can be kept in a closed container for a long time. Plop them at the kitchen table with some cookie cutters and a small rolling pin and let them have fun.

Window Crayons/Markers–When they were old enough not to draw where they shouldn't, we used window crayons or markers to decorate the sliding back door for Hon.

Tip: My Favorite Playdough Recipe

Mix all the ingredients in a saucepan and stir over medium heat for three to five minutes until the mixture thickens. You can also add flavors like lemon, but I don't recommend brown ones like vanilla or root beer as they create dingy playdough.

- 2 tablespoons cooking oil
- 4 tablespoons cream of tartar
- 2 cups plain flour
- 1 cup salt
- Food coloring
- 2 cups water

Little Boy Boundaries

My boys needed regular reminders of basic rules like "Don't hit your brother" or "Let someone else have a turn." Occasionally, behavior deteriorated to a firmer message, and a time-out was needed. Time-outs come in all different forms. When the kids were little, nap time was really "Momma needed some time-out." With two boys, play often got carried away, ending with somebody crying or hurt. I did not like being a warden, forcing the boys to stay in a chair or not leave their bedroom, so I often put the boys' favorite toy into time-out on top of the refrigerator. Removing their toy and putting it out of reach typically did the trick, and once things calmed down, the toy would be returned.

Time-out worked well as they became older too. There was always some coveted item or activity that could be taken away when they were teenagers. Computers, cell phones, and car keys all had their time in the penalty box when the rules of the house were broken.

Emotional Reinforcement

The MOB friends I bonded with tackled some tough issues over the years and discussed and shared a wide variety of opinions and experiences. The honest discussions were invaluable to me as I learned how to be a mother. Of course, there was a bit of venting too as there's nothing that bonds like shared experiences.

There is an endless library of books from experts on raising children and boys. When Earnest was in first grade, I felt very inadequate and was looking for help. I was a very busy mom, juggling home, kids, and work, and had no time for life balance. I searched for a resource that might help me and found a documentary: *Raising Cain: Exploring the Inner Lives of America's Boys* by Michael G. Thompson PhD. I got so much out of it that I invited other mothers of boys that I knew over to have a pot of chili and watch the documentary. Hour one was from birth to middle school, and hour two was from middle school through high school. I always got new tips when I watched it because the boys were in different stages of development, but the conversations and sharing of experiences with the MOB were as valuable as the documentary.

Case in point: I struggled with Earnest in first grade because I was comparing him to other kids in the class. This was not helpful, especially when comparing him to girls of the same age. Discussions with the MOB helped me be less critical of myself and him because we were all struggling with similar things.

After watching the documentary, reading other parenting books, and talking with the MOB, I realized that there were many times when I did not slow down to listen to my boys. I learned to pause long enough to let them try to express themselves. Also, helping my boys learn how to communicate using their words and recognize their emotions was one of the most critical and beneficial things I did as a parent.

Another aha moment for me was appreciating the boys *are* emotional and needed emotional reinforcement that I heard them or their attention-seeking actions would escalate. I grew up in a "buck up" time for males when emotions like crying were discouraged. With my boys, I focused on getting them to talk and express what was bothering them. When they were young, I'd lie in their bed as they went to sleep and talk with them. It was a time of day when I was not so stressed and was better able to listen and give them the emotional support and the reinforcement they needed.

The Imagination Factory

There were very active imaginations in our house, and the boys were born storytellers. They thoroughly enjoyed sharing imaginary adventures with friends. I was sad when this stage was over and recommend you capture some of your favorite tales. Here are a few:

"Grandfader"

Earnest had "Grandfader," an older man who would tell him great stories, let him use his computer, and take him on adventures. Grandfader would take him on hikes behind our house where they spotted rare animals and plants. Then they would go to the B&O Railroad Museum and climb all over the trains. At one point, Earnest started pointing out a house on our street where Grandfader lived. His stories had become so convincing that we began to wonder if the person was real, but since he was four and was never alone, logic and good sense prevailed.

We had asked Earnest if he was talking about Pop or PopPop, and he always looked at us like we were the ones confused. He knew who his grandfathers were. He confidently stressed that this was *Grandfader*. It's quite humbling when a child sets you straight.

Earnest's stories had a familiar ring to me as they were the adventures that I had with my grandfather, Poppy. Poppy was one of a kind. He was a travel writer and traversed the world and wrote about his adventures for the *Washington Herald* in DC. When he returned from an adventure, he would share a slide show and narrate his travels. It was like having a front-row seat at the *National Geographic*. His stories were often a weave of fact, fiction, and humor, and it was hard to know where the facts ended and the fiction began. Poppy had his own museum with relics collected on his adventures. I remember the wooden teeth from George Washington; the small derringer that shot Lincoln; a bell from Rudolph's harness; and a large wooden noisemaker that was swung over the head of a crew member on a barge, sounding the alarm in the fog. His adventures had to be true because he had the museum items as proof! Earnest's stories felt like those I had been told as a child.

One night, my cousin came to visit, and I asked Earnest to tell her about Grandfader. With a captive audience, Earnest happily launched into storytelling mode. When he was done, I asked my cousin what she thought.

"That's Poppy, isn't it?" she said with smiling eyes.

I agreed. We knew if anyone was going to come back and visit the next generation, it would surely be our Poppy. Earnest's adventures with Grandfader lasted until he was about five. The stories slowly faded with time and, sadly for me, came to an end.

"*Charlie and Patricks*"

Exuberance had imaginary brothers. Apparently, Earnest was not enough, so along came Charlie. Charlie had red hair, was in his twenties, and was in the army. He fought in the war, and his weapons seemed to jump time periods as he battled bad guys with swords and guns. Exuberance and Charlie would leap, climb, and slay dragons around his room. Sometimes Charlie got too excited and broke things. Exuberance couldn't be held responsible for Charlie's rambunctiousness! At some point, Charlie went back to the war, and Patricks arrived. Yes, Patricks was always pronounced with an *s*. Patricks had green hair and was a soldier. Occasionally, Exuberance, Charlie, and Patricks went off to war and fought in great battles. These stories were very detailed and usually included much diving, stabbings, and rolling around when retold.

Exuberance became a hit at nursery school. All the male classmates, with a tinge of jealousy, knew of his imaginary brothers, Charlie and Patricks. Sometimes, Charlie and Patricks would return from battle missing limbs and very much *bloody*. This was not disturbing at all for Exuberance, and he thought it was cool that their wounds would be miraculously healed in time for the next story. Exuberance's imaginary brothers hung around until first grade when his attention turned to lacrosse. When I ask him about them today, he still remembers those brothers vividly and fondly.

In my heart, I believe their imaginary friends are souls finding their way to heaven. Neither boy was ever scared by their presence, and I think their imaginary friends provided comfort in a world where reality can often be overwhelming. Embracing these moments and enjoying the stories worked well for us. As the boys matured, reality won the battle over make-believe, and the imaginary friends faded away.

A New Member of the Family

I had a poop quota and refused to get a dog until everyone was out of diapers. Exuberance, then three, took the challenge seriously and stopped pooping. He was good about peeing in the toilet, but pooping was a different story. He woke up in the middle of the night, wailing because he was constipated. "You have a diaper on. Poop in the diaper or poop in the toilet." But no, he was too stubborn to do either and just kept crying in pain.

"Hon, I think we need to take him to the emergency room to get an enema!"

"Absolutely not," said Hon. "I'll get him to poop!" The two of them retreated to the downstairs bathroom where much crying and shouting occurred.

"Get out. I'll do it," said Exuberance.

Hon waited near the bathroom door. After a *long* time, the door opened, and mission accomplished. "I'm going to bed," said Exuberance.

Since everyone was potty trained, it was time to get a dog. A beautiful, sweet English Setter puppy came to live with us. It was good to have another female in the house! We named her Razel. Razel was a nickname my grandfather, Poppy, used to call cute women in his neighborhood when he went on walks with my brother and me. I assumed it meant cute female since that's how he seemed to use it. But now that we had just named the puppy Razel, I was worried

Earnest, Exuberance, and Razel enjoy balls, sticks, bugs, and dirt.

that it could mean anything. I nervously looked it up on the internet and was relieved to read that it is a Yiddish word meaning "unconditional love" or "rose." What a perfect name for our puppy!

Razel and the boys loved the same things—sticks, critters, balls, tug of war, and chase. They were busy together. Razel was a "letter of the law" kind of girl. She knew she could not jump on people, so she would dance and lean on you. She was bigger than Exuberance, and in no time, she decided he was her puppy. There was a short period when Razel slept in Exuberance's bed. One morning, she growled at me when I woke them up for preschool. Razel and I had a conversation about the growl, and that wasn't going to fly. I got her a dog bed, and that was the end of sleeping with the boys.

Brotherly Love

I was well aware of the bruises that come with brotherly love, having been dearly loved by my brother. For those unfamiliar with these rough-and-tumble displays of affection, romping and roughhousing is their love language.

There was a period when Exuberance was becoming a regular at the emergency room for stitches and surgical glue. These trips were not always Earnest's fault, as his little brother was fully capable of hurling himself at objects like a superhero. Hon and I would rock-paper-scissors these "fun" parental experiences.

The cause of one of these ER visits was a typical boy's risk-blind brilliance. Earnest had Exuberance in a hammock and was trying to flip him all the way around while Razel circled and barked in

> **Tip: Memory**
>
> I was often amazed at how quickly the boys and their friend got over something. They would get in a fight, hit each other, and ten minutes later, laugh as though nothing ever happened.
>
> As a mom, I had to remember that my memory was more mature than theirs and avoid getting sucked into the short-lived drama.

excitement. Exuberance only made it halfway around before gravity took over and dropped him on the metal hammock pole. The metal pole left a lightning bolt-shaped gash on his forehead, which an astute ER doc identified as a Harry Potter scar. The crying immediately stopped upon that realization, and a quality battle wound was born.

As the boys grew, their "brother love" could spark intense "I've had enough" loud moments. Stomping, slamming doors, shoving, and punching were all possible during these times. I did not like being a referee and did everything I could to make them figure out how to resolve the issue for themselves. My go-to statement for these skirmishes was, "Figure it out, or I'll figure it out, and no one will be happy!"

Tip: The size of the bandage needs to match the *perceived* level of pain.

I give new mothers of boys a box of superhero Band-Aids and an ace bandage. When faced with a little man down and a *bloody* event, stay calm and bandage up. The Band-Aid proves the injury happened, and when needed, wrapping up a limb in an Ace bandage becomes an opportunity to show off battle scars that match their perceived level of pain and injury.

Exuberance, the king of the loopholes, once wore his Ace-bandaged arm to elementary school. I was flagged down by the teacher when I picked him up and was asked, "When would he be able to write again?" Apparently, he was too wounded to practice his letters. "Tomorrow!" I answered.

Caregivers

As a video producer, I was very familiar with doing research and often had the opportunity to interview experts. Before I became pregnant, I produced a new baby video for a local healthcare system, watched several births, interviewed lactation specialists, and demonstrated step-by-step how to install a car seat correctly. While I was pregnant, I produced a video on the difference between licensed center-based daycares and home-based daycares. In our state, there is a database of licensed daycare providers that you can access by zip code.

Hon and I selected home daycare solutions for the boys. We discovered some incredible licensed daycare providers from the state-supplied list, and those women played a critical role in the development of our boys. These carefully chosen environments helped the boys become socialized with other children and were the building blocks of their resilience. I will forever be grateful to the women who helped care for my boys and were part of the love and encouragement that helped them become happy adults.

Sister Sense—Day Care

There are so many variables when it comes to daycare: the caregiver, location, your child, other children, your job commitments, and more. Consider it a success if your daycare works longer than six-months.

Weather Mom

I was the weather forecaster for our family. After checking the three-legged stool philosophy's basics of food, exercise, and sleep, I'd refer to my knowledge of historical patterns and find myself predicting the day: A sunny morning with a chance of a forgotten lunch box.

As a Weather Mom, I would never be able to change Earnest and Exuberance, or Hon for that matter. My job was to put up the kid-friendly bumpers in the bowling alley of life, so they might traverse the day and knock down a few pins.

The Weather Mom knew when the sun was shining to go out and play! And when it was stormy, to batten the hatches and watch a movie like *Sandlot* or any version of *Peter Pan*. The Weather Mom's job was to skip down the road on sunny days and slow down on rainy ones.

The Weather Mom was also in charge of the schedules. In our family, I was the one who looked into the future to predict and understand our schedules. Hon and the boys were oblivious to doctors' appointments, holidays, and vacations. Looking back, I should have done a better job of communicating with Hon and making him more active in the mental load I was taking on with juggling the family. I was an early adopter of computer calendars and set up a separate calendar on Google for each boy and myself in different colors. Juggling sports schedules, activities, and my job would never have been possible without Dr. Google reminding me of what was next in my day as the Weather Mom.

> **Tip: Splish, Splash, They Were Taking a Bath**
>
> A bathtub is a toddler mom's best friend! As the boys got older and showered on their own, it become impressive how much water they could get outside of the tub, flooding the bathroom floor. This issue was resolved by hiring a glass installer to add a one-foot wide by five-feet tall piece of shatterproof glass attached to the top of tub and the wall nearest the faucet. I have made this modification in multiple houses and found it more functional than sliding doors on the tub.

Nursery School

Both boys went to a co-op nursery school at a nearby church. Earnest started when he was four, and Exuberance attended from three and four. Those nursery school years were pivotal in teaching them how to make new friends and listen to the teacher.

What I didn't realize at the time was that I got more out of those nursery school years than they did! I learned how to volunteer. As a co-op school, all the parents had to volunteer and attend a few educational lectures during the school year. When it came to volunteering, my strategy was to get in there early and pick something that either had a specific period of time that I could accomplish quickly or find something that I enjoyed doing, like taking pictures of the kids.

Nursery school also taught me how important it is to have mother-friends. They were my first MOB, and I am still close with many of the mothers. There were several families that had two kids the same age as the boys, so the moms spent three years together during that nursery school period.

Out 'n' Backs

My mom used to call an *out 'n' back*,[5] a quick trip to do something, and they were always much more appealing than running an errand. There were some days when the boys were little that we just needed a change of scenery. Here are some of our favorite out 'n' back and fun activities:
- We loved going to a park or playground.
- We lived near an airport and often went to watch the planes land.
- A zoo of any size is a winner!
- Visit a construction site or any large piece of equipment. The boys loved construction equipment so much that we had a video of land being cleared with giant bulldozers and diggers. It was one of their favorites!
- Celebrate the garbage men. It's so fun to watch the boys tear out of the house to wave to the garbage truck, and the workers love it too.

---

[5] Out 'n' backs: a nickname for running errands. Sounds a lot more fun, right?

- Visit a fire station. Another win-win experience.
- Go to a farm and pick anything—strawberries, pumpkins, apples.

> ### Tip: Halloween, Tax, and Giving
>
> If there was ever a holiday made for boys, it is Halloween! Our costumes always seemed to center around superheroes, firemen and policemen, and anything with a weapon or magic wand. Hon and I used to call houses with fantastic decorations for Halloween and Christmas overachievers since we never seemed to have the time or energy to be competitive. Exuberance heard *over retrievers*, and would scream whenever he saw a *boney*, a.k.a. a skeleton, and shout, "Look an over retriever."
>
> The amount of candy that comes into your house at Halloween is ridiculous and fair game. Our boys understood there was a tax on Halloween candy that parents appropriated. It was one of their first lessons on economics. I recommend making three piles of candy: the child's favorite, parent tax, and donation. Soldiers were our favorite group to donate candy to, and it was a gateway opportunity to think and talk about the needs of others.

Mudder's Day

Mother's Day is good in theory but stressful in practice. It should really be called "It's Your Turn, Fathers!" After decades of Mother's Day, I suggest setting your expectations low, have your humor ready, and write it down so it can be a continued source of entertainment. Here's one of my funniest Mother's Days.

I awaken to notice that Hon is up. I peek at the clock: 7:30 a.m. Maybe no one will notice I'm not around. I close my eyes. My nose wakes me this time. Coffee. That's odd. I'm the only coffee drinker in the house. I listen. It's too quiet. Oh, it's Mother's Day. I look at the clock again: 8:50 a.m. I think they'd better wake me up soon, or we won't make it to church on time. I listen at the top of the stairs. There are great activities below; they're coming. I run back to bed.

Earnest, almost six, and Exuberance, age four, bound into the room with homemade cards. Earnest's card says, "Happy Mudders Day! I love you."

Exuberance's card says, "I like your heart." He also points out that he has written "007" on the back. Charlie, his invisible brother, has taught him to write. OK then.

Earnest brings in a present he made in kindergarten. It's a recipe book. I gather everything together and herd the boys downstairs. Daddy's feeling left out.

Hon has gone out and bought a variety of sugar and chocolate-covered donuts. He also made a valiant attempt to brew coffee. I pour myself a cup. It's nuclear and takes quite a bit of cream to make it the right color. I begin to page through the recipe book; all the recipes are from mothers in Earnest's class. I think I don't remember being asked for a recipe and then came across mine:

My Mom's Homemade Syrup

Ingredients:
½ of a bottle of regular syrup
Sugar

Directions:
1. Pour four gallons of sugar into the bottle of syrup
2. Put it into the microwave
3. Cook in the microwave for thirteen hours
4. Pour over waffles and pancakes

Things are making slightly more sense now. *All* the recipes were made up by the kindergarteners. Maybe it's the nuclear coffee I'm drinking. I grab some clothes for the boys and head back upstairs to get ready, singing, "You Make Me Feel So Young," in the shower. Upon finishing, I decide I don't look too bad. I bothered to put in my contacts, have some nice black pants on recently de-linted of white dog hair and pollen, and a funky shirt. I'm ready for church.

Church is relatively uneventful for a change. Earnest decided to go to the nursery, so the odds are, with Hon and me, two adults to one boy. We sneak out early to go to my parent's house. The plan is to meet them, my brother and his family, for brunch. We've already purchased the traditional Mother's Day rose bush for Mom, so we're going to drop by their house first.

We're loading the kids into the car when Earnest tells us his stomach hurts. Hon asks him when the last time he'd gone to the bathroom. I'm suspicious of the popcorn from the night before and the chocolate donuts for breakfast. After a trip back into the church to the bathroom, we decide it's safe to continue our day.

After paying the toll at the Harbor Tunnel, I notice Earnest is crying in the back seat. "Are you going to throw up?" He nods. Hon pulls over on a minuscule shoulder at the mouth of the tunnel. I hand Earnest Exuberance's handy vampire cape, which is in the back seat, to get sick in. He does. Hon pulls him out of the car and rushes him to the guardrail.

Exuberance is sobbing. "My cape!"

I try to get out of the car and bang the door into the guardrail. Quite a christening for Hon's two-week-old car. He yells at me about the door and grabs some towels from the back. My arm is covered in puke from the initial cape incident. Earnest has thrown up on his shirt and pants. I pull off his shirt and wrap a towel around him. He's feeling better then. We're off again through the tunnel. No way to turn around; might as well go forward.

Exuberance continues to cry in the back seat. Earnest is looking green. Hon and I are discussing our options. Earnest starts crying again. We pull over.

Exuberance cries on and off. "Why does Earnest get to throw up? I want to throw up too." Exuberance has just taken jealousy to a new level!

Earnest tries to explain that it burns. "It's spicy!"

Exuberance wants to get in on the fun and begins to cough and gag until Hon yells at him to stop. During all of this, I remember one of my mom's tips: "Don't argue. Distract."

I look at Earnest and say, "Do you have a loose tooth?" His entire attitude changes briefly when he realizes that he will soon be losing his first tooth although it doesn't keep him from throwing up a few more times before we reach Mom and Dad's. It's twelve forty-five, and we were supposed to be at brunch by twelve thirty. I can just imagine the conversation at the table. Of course, Hon and I forgot to bring our cell phones.

I race Earnest into the house where he throws up again. I put him in one of Pop's T-shirts, washed my hands, and put him on the couch. Hon's now at the front door, asking where I am. I run out and jump in the car with Exuberance, and we head off to the restaurant, leaving Earnest and Hon at the house.

We arrived for brunch over thirty minutes late. Exuberance and I wash our hands again before finding the gang. I plop Exuberance at the table, make quick exclamations to my mom, and run off to get him some food at the buffet. After getting myself a plate of food, I return to sit in between Mom and my bro, in front of a bloody Mary. Thank God!

Bro leans over, laughing, and says, "You should have heard her," with a nod at Mom, which means there was much commentary regarding our tardiness. Mom says she was just worried about us.

Bro decides to take all the kids on an "adventure to see the sharks." The restaurant has a small fishpond outside, and I think my how the goldfish have grown. Exuberance has his cousin Em, who is the same age, by his hand and explains that they are going to get married. Em beams, and Ry, who's two years older, tries to explain to an unresponsive audience that cousins can't marry.

Em and Exuberance ride with me back to Mom and Dad's house. The conversation is in full force before getting out of the parking lot. Em's talking about an impending sleepover, and Exuberance explains that he's not afraid of the dark anymore because Charlie and Patricks are with him. I tell Em that they're Exuberance's invisible brothers. "Oh, sure," she says. I think she'll be getting some soon.

We all head home a bit later, and within five minutes of the ride, I'm holding Earnest by the waist while he throws up on the side of the road. Exuberance is not jealous anymore. We toss the car seat in the back, lay Earnest down, and boogie home. It's about this time that I take a look at myself. My pants are covered in lint and dog hair again, my contacts feel like sandpaper, and I smell like puke. I think I always have some song in my head. They sort of underscore my life, and one of my favorites from *West Side Story* starts, "I feel pretty ... oh, so pretty."

We finally make it home and everyone crashes for a mandatory nap. Hon and I order pizza, and our neighbors invite us to eat and drink with them on their deck. After a big chocolate and yogurt kiss on my cheek from each boy, it seems this Mudders Day is one for the memory books.

Slow-Rolling Jokes

Foxy Loxy

Let's face it, little kids are gullible, which can be a lot of fun. Parents get to be the Tooth Fairy, Easter Bunny, and Santa Claus. In our family, we love slow roller jokes, the kind of joke that might take years for the kids to get. These gems get planted young and are discussed regularly so they're not forgotten.

My grandfather, Poppy, was the king of the storytellers. He had the most incredible sense of humor, and his grandchildren were a captive audience. Poppy wrote a newspaper travel column in DC. I still think that had to be one of the coolest jobs, to be paid to travel around the world and write about it! In addition to being a professional storyteller, he was the master of the slow-rolling joke.

It was always an adventure when Nana and Poppy came to visit. Poppy loved to take us on hikes, which he called Foxy Loxys. He had a good friend, Roland Q. Fox, who we would look for in the woods. As Poppy shuffled along, he would teach us about the plants in the woods and quiz us on things like the Latin name for skunk cabbage. Looking back as an adult, I realize that whenever we got too far ahead of him, he spotted Foxy Loxy.

"There he is!" he'd shout.

We'd come romping back, "Where?"

"Sorry. I said hello, and then he ran off," he would say. I have many wonderful memories of those hikes, looking for Foxy Loxy and making terrariums out of moss and small plants we found in the woods.

Poppy passed away when I was a freshman in high school. There was a service for him in DC, and his friends came from far and wide. After the service, his five grandchildren, ranging in ages from thirteen to seventeen, stood together in line to greet people on the way out. A man came up to us and said, "I was a very good friend of your grandfather's. My name is Roland Q. Fox." The five of us stood there with our mouths open, totally dumbstruck. Just when we knew Foxy Loxy wasn't real, there he was, standing in front of us. Yes, Poppy always got the last laugh.

Off Like a Herd of Turtles!

Hon used to announce as everyone loaded into the car, "Off like a herd of turtles." I think Earnest was about eight when he said, "Dad, I don't think turtles are very fast." When he realized he'd uncovered the slow-rolling joke, he beamed from ear to ear.

I was always challenging myself to make up slow-rolling jokes when the kids were little. The road to visit my parents was full of slow-rolling joke opportunities and imagination. Living near Baltimore,

Maryland, we had to travel forty-five minutes north to Mom and Dad's. As we crossed the Francis Scott Key Bridge over the Patapsco River, I'd point out our Neverland from *Peter Pan*. It was actually an abandoned and overgrown fort built to protect the Baltimore Harbor and Fort McHenry in the middle of the river, Fort Carroll. Sometimes, if we really tried, we'd spot Captain Hook's pirate ship coming around the point. Everyone would crane their necks on the bridge to look for pirate ships. Earnest always saw Captain Hook, which made Exuberance mad.

Further up the highway were two large gold-colored domes, also known locally as the Golden Eggs. Earnest wanted to know what they were, and I told him that they were the king and queen's throne. Years later, as we drove by, Earnest asked, "What king lives there?" When I explained that it was really a sewage treatment plant and told him a toilet's nickname is a throne, he almost busted a gut laughing. It was a very slow-rolling joke that I'd been enjoying for years.

Hon's cousin Bo taught his kids to yell, "Come in," whenever someone toots. It was so fun, we adopted it too. I wish I was a fly on the wall in middle school when they shout out "Come in" and realize it may not be an appropriate response to a fart. Or is it?

Goody Goody the First of May

My mom is also a champion in the slow-rolling joke category. All my life, on May 1, there was a competition with my mom's sister and her family to see who could be the first to say, "Goody, goody, the first of May."

When I was a kid, my mom would bounce in to wake us up, exclaiming, "Goody, goody, the first of May!" The phone would ring, and my aunt or cousin would shout it into the phone and then hang up. Great laughter and bragging rights always surrounded May Day.

Telephones were *finally* installed in our dorm rooms during my junior year of college. That May Day the phone rang early, jolting my roommate and me out of bed. My roommate tossed me the phone. It was my mom.

"Goody, goody, the first of May. Outdoor screwing begins today!" *Click.*

I was stunned. I called back and managed to spit out while laughing my head off, "Mom, where did the second part of that saying come from?"

"Oh, you're finally old enough to know the rest," said Mom.

Goody, goody, the first of May is still a thing; my mom is the champion, and the boys, now in their twenties, enjoy the joke too.

Tip: Fun Birthday Party Activity and Party Favor

The key to a boy activity is that it needs to be short and simple. We had several parties over the years where we tie-dyed T-shirts.

- Pack of white T-shirts.
- Mix two or three kid selected fabric dyes in separate buckets.
- Pack of rubber bands.
- Old plastic grocery bags or large Ziploc bags.
- Get kids to pucker shirts with rubber bands.
- Dip parts or whole shirts in buckets of colored dye.
- Put the dyed shirt in a plastic grocery bag with their name written on it. Tie it tight and send with directions to rinse and wash after a few hours or the next day.

Time for Romance? Ha!

Finding kid-free moments to catch up and talk with Hon was a struggle as we juggled young kids, family, and work. One weekend, our neighbor, Rose, told me to take advantage of their hot tub while they were out of town. Their house was very close to ours, and their hot tub was feet from our deck and backyard. Rose had raised three boys and knew how important it was to squeeze in adult time.

I pitched the idea to Hon, and he was all in. The boys were about four and six, and Razel was around a year old. After putting the boys to bed, we stashed Razel in her crate and slipped next door in our bathing suits to take advantage of the hot tub. It was heaven after a long week of work, and it was wonderful to catch up.

Suddenly, I noticed that Razel was running around the backyard. She was pretty good at escaping, but I knew she couldn't manage opening doors. "Hon, how do you think Razel got out?" We looked at the back of our house with the screen door open.

"I'll check it out." Hon grabbed his towel and headed to the back of the house with Razel dancing around him. I continued to soak. Several minutes passed, and he did not return. I finally climbed out of the hot tub to find out what the delay was.

When I walked in, Earnest turned to me with a look of conflicted concern. Apparently, Razel had woken him up crying about being forced to get in her crate and go to bed early. When Earnest came down, he let Razel out and discovered no parents in the house. He then became worried and ran out the front door to knock on Rose and Kerry's front door. Realizing they were not home, he ran back and knew just what to do. That year in nursery school, he learned about calling 911 in an emergency, and in his assessment, this fitted the bill. He picked up the phone to report his missing parents. Earnest was on the phone with the operator when Hon walked in the back screen door and asked, "What's going on, Earnest? Who are you talking to?"

"Uh ... uh ... I couldn't find you," he said, handing Hon the phone.

Hon realized what was happening and tried to explain the confusion and that no one was in danger. The operator told him she understood, but they had to send an officer for a welfare check and to investigate. When I walked in, Hon was at the front door, a towel wrapped around his waist, talking to a police officer. Assessing that all was well and having a good chuckle, the officer told Earnest he did a good job and went on his way.

We told Earnest that he did nothing wrong and decided to blame the whole event on Razel. Earnest, tired from protecting the house, was taken to bed. Exuberance slept through the entire thing, and Hon and I learned our lesson about trying to squeeze in a romantic moment without planning and lining up a babysitter.

> ### Tip: The Tooth Fairy
>
> Baby teeth seem to fall out when you have no cash in the house, are on vacation, or out of town. Kids love the magic of waking up with a few quarters or a dollar under their pillow, but it's hard to remember to be the tooth fairy after a dozen teeth. Earnest would sulk down the stairs in disappointment that the tooth fairy didn't show up. "Really? Let's check again," I'd say as I dropped a dollar on the floor and kicked it under the bed. "Maybe you tossed and turned in your sleep, and it fell?"
>
> Hon also created a five o'clock rule where if your tooth fell out after 5:00 p.m., the Tooth Fairy's route had already been set, and you'd be put on the next day's schedule. We obviously did not always have our act together, but we're pretty good at covering our tracks!

The Cowboy Way

How do you teach respect and chivalry to a young male? This is a tough nut to crack, but when it happens, it's gold. Once we took a trip to Durango, Colorado, and met the most wonderful man, Cowboy Ben. He looked as though he had walked off the set of a cowboy movie with his hat, boots, and belt buckle. Earnest and Exuberance were enthralled. This was a man who demanded respect and gave it to even the youngest of kids. He had the golden goo.

Cowboy Ben had a chat with the boys about how to be respectful, "Listen to your momma," and say, "Yes, ma'am." This was followed by "Treat women with kindness," "Hold open the door," and "Do not raise your hand to strike another unless in defense." The man had an amazing way with the boys.

Cowboy Ben told them a classic story about his son. At his son's high school graduation, a female classmate came up to him and his wife and told them that their son was a true gentleman. Apparently, one day during class, the girl passed gas loudly. His son raised his hand quickly and said, "Excuse me," to the whole class. He took the blame for the gaseous explosion. I could see Earnest and Exuberance processing what a valiant move this was. A true act of heroism to accept the blame for a fart the cowboy way. You never know where role models will pop up, and for me, a cowboy was just perfect. Thank you, Cowboy Ben.

Tip: The Number of Friends Invited to a Birthday Party

Birthday parties can become a competitive event in some communities, and I recommend keeping it simple. We tried to keep the number of the partygoers equal to the boy's age plus family.

A smaller guest list gives you more flexibility for fun and party favors. One of our best birthday parties included a squirt gun favor. Buckets of water were placed around the yard, and a water battle ensued. The big boys, a.k.a. Dads, love it too. I will never forget my brother holding his three-year-old daughter in front of him as a shield while he fired at the seven-year-old boys. Good times.

Somebody Else's Shoes

Teaching and living with empathy in your heart is not necessarily intuitive. "You can't understand someone until you've walked a mile in their shoes," and the Golden Rule, "Do unto others as you would have others do unto you"—these have all always resonated with me. It was important for me to remember that you don't know what's going on in another person's home. Trying to understand *why* a child or adult behaved in a certain way served me well before I reacted.

Your patience with how other children and adults treat your child will be tested as a mom. It's essential to accept that you will probably not have all the facts from your child when presented with issues and concerns. Your child and others involved will often skip facts that are not flattering or embarrassing. The momma bear side of your brain will want to dash in to protect your son when a coach or another child picks on them. Occasionally, momma bear is warranted, but a more measured approach will usually yield better results.

In live television, back when profanity was unheard of on TV, there was a seven-second delay between what was live in the studio and what was broadcasted. The delay allowed the audio engineer to insert a bleep over a cuss word that might have slipped out. I tried to practice the seven-second delay during trying parenting times as a tool to keep my cool and speak with authority. It's amazing how a few moments can change your response.

Kids do not know what they don't know. Maybe they weren't taught the same values as your children. There will be lots of opportunities to correct other people's children. It's critical to try to keep kindness in your heart when you are talking with children. I recommend getting physically down to their level, looking them in the eyes, and trying to understand, not criticizing them. Taking the time to gain a child's trust before you offer recommendations or small course corrections will get you far!

> **Sister Sense—Little Kid Sports**
>
> Sign the boys up for timed sports, sports that have a time clock like basketball, soccer, and lacrosse. Sports like baseball and meet sports like swimming, track, wrestling and gymnastics can last all day.
>
> When the boys were little, they tried karate, soccer, baseball, and lacrosse. There is nothing as slow as a little kid baseball game, and nothing as funny as the dusty dirt pile of kids chasing a soccer ball, just happy that they are in the pack.

A Picky Eater

Getting a picky eater to expand his palate and eat healthier was a puzzle that I never solved. Earnest started life as a great eater, but something changed around age three. He had giant tonsils and huge taste buds. Food would get stuck, and he'd gag if he didn't chew his food well. Dr. B and I had many conversations about his eating.

"Dr. B, I think he must have strep throat!"

"Why do you think that?" he'd ask.

"Look at the blisters on the back of his tongue."

"Those aren't blisters. They're taste buds."

"Good grief! No wonder his favorite food is mashed potatoes!"

The ear, nose, and throat doctor said that Earnest didn't have kissing tonsils, he had hugging tonsils. They were huge!

"Can't we have them taken out? I had my tonsils taken out."

"We don't do that anymore unless there's an issue of repeated strep throat," said the specialists.

Strep throat was not our issue. "What about sleep apnea? I slept in the same bed with Earnest one night on vacation. He was snoring like a banshee and didn't seem to sleep well." The sleep apnea issue worked, and out came the tonsils.

Removing Earnest's tonsils fixed the snore and gag issues but not his sensitivity to texture and taste. Hon, who grew up in a big family, couldn't wrap his head around Earnest refusing to eat the food that was prepared for him. Earnest was always so kind as he refused, "No, thank you," with a waved hand. He just wouldn't eat, making the first leg of the three-legged stool philosophy very wobbly and an energy-sapped little boy. I couldn't take it and would make him something bland to eat. I think he survived on peanut butter sandwiches on wheat bread as a little boy. I even took him to a child behavior specialist, who, after many sessions of trying to convince Earnest to eat cereal with milk, said to me, "He'll probably grow out of it." He didn't. Earnest learned to cook for himself by fifth grade. I finally exclaimed, "I'm not a short-order cook. I make one meal. If you don't like it, make yourself something else," and so he did. In his twenties, Earnest got COVID-19, lost his taste, and tried sushi. LOL.

> ### Sister Sense—Face Dinners
>
> A friend shared that when her kids were little and she had zero gas in the tank at dinner time (often!), her family would have "Face Dinners" and create faces on their plates with food.
>
> She would fill little bowls with all kinds of different food cut in different shapes. The bowls might include circles of cucumbers for eyes, round cherry tomatoes for earrings, raisins for freckles, cooked pasta and shredded cheese for hair. The family could use these ingredients as art supplies to make a face on the plate. The kids thought it was a blast and it saved her from cooking a big meal on a hectic day.

Recipe: Sugar and Cinnamon Donuts

My mom used to pass these around at Halloween with apple cider when we were kids. This was one of Earnest's favorite weekend breakfasts to make with me.

Ingredients

- Refrigerator biscuits ("Grands" are not necessary, the little ones in the round tube work great.)
- Vegetable oil
- Sugar and cinnamon

Directions

Pour about two or three inches of vegetable oil into a pot on medium heat. Spread the biscuits on a cutting board and find something round to cut a hole in the center. We took the rubber top off the turkey baster and used the stem to make holes in the dough. Use one of the holes to test if the oil is hot enough. Once the oil is hot, use tongs to slowly put the dough in the oil. Flip them until the dough is medium brown. Lay cooked donuts on paper towels to remove excess oil. Mix sugar and cinnamon in a container with a lid or lunch bag. Add the donuts a few at a time and shake to coat. (The boys were excellent shakers.)

I stored the cooled donut oil in a mason jar in the refrigerator for the next cooking opportunity.

Elementary School

The more that you read, the more things you will know.
The more that you learn, the more places you'll go.
—Dr. Seuss, *I Can Read with My Eyes Shut!*

Starting School

Elementary school was a challenge for our wiggly boys. One of my biggest takeaways was that I needed to be their advocate and make sure I communicated effectively with teachers and staff. I always remained calm and respectful, but when I needed to, I brought in Hon or educational experts/teacher friends to back me up and support my child.

Figuring out how to support the boys and help them become better students was tricky. Acting out in school was often a sign that they were behind and uncomfortable with what was being taught. During those times, Hon and I had to take a step back and brainstorm realistic solutions. We leaned heavily on professionals and tutors during those times.

Help from professionals began when Earnest was in kindergarten and could not hold his pencil in what was deemed the correct way. His fine motor skills were delayed and an occupational therapist came to our house to help him. We always started our search for professionals with our pediatrician, who was a critical resource. (FYI: Earnest still doesn't hold his pencil correctly, but it didn't seem to have slowed down his career in information technology and cyber security.)

We had several ridiculous interactions with the principal at our local elementary school when Earnest was in first and second grade. Here are some of the stories from that time.

Standing in Line

I'm not sure there was a greater torture for my boys in elementary school than to have to stand in line. Earnest's school had the kids wait outside the school in line before the morning bell. The first call I received from the principal occurred after a standing-in-line incident when Earnest was in first grade.

Earnest was bumping a friend in line when the kid turned around and kneed Earnest in the crotch. He went down and was taken to the school nurse. The principal called me in distress and asked me to come into the school.

The principal, the two boys, and I sat in a small conference room. I waited for the principal to get the conversation started. When she didn't, I said, "OK, boys, what happened?" The boys explained the rough play gone bad exchange. With no response from the principal, I continued, "Did you realize that a knee in the crotch would hurt that badly?"

Both boys nodded no. "I remember doing something like that to my brother once, and I was surprised at how much it hurt him and never did it again. Now that you understand, will you do it again?"

Both boys shook their heads no. "Well then, apologize and shake hands." The boys apologized and shook hands. I look back at the radio-silent principal. "Can they go back to class now?" I asked.

"Yes," she finally said. Off they went.

I turned to her and asked, "Are we good now? May I go back to work?"

The principal said, "Yes. Wow! You're really good at this!"

I thought, "Wow! You're really not!"

Another Missed Teaching Opportunity

During another first-grade incident, the principal called me to tell me that Earnest had brought my bra into school in his lunch bag. "Huh," I thought. "I only have two, and I have one on." I was at a business lunch and was not impressed with the principal after the prior standing-in-line incident. It was like boys were a new species to her. "OK. Tell Earnest to go back to class, and my husband or I will be there as soon as we can to talk about it."

I called Hon. Maybe he'd have better luck with the principal, and besides, it was his turn. Hon was not thrilled to be asked to leave work early to retrieve my bra and Earnest, but he wrapped up his day and headed to the elementary school. Earnest was in total tears, traumatized from the perceived trouble he was in with the principal and was in the nurse's office because he couldn't stop crying in his classroom.

Hon and Earnest sat in the principal's office. "What happened?" Hon asked Earnest.

Earnest explained, "My friend and I were having lunch. He had potato chips. I told him I had my mom's bra in my lunch bag, and I'd trade him for some chips. There was a girl at our table, and she told the lunch monitor that I had my mom's bra."

Hon turns to the principal, "May I have the bra?"

The principal says, "There wasn't one. He made it up."

Hon stared at her in disbelief. "I left work to pick up our son early from school because he is an immature joke teller?" He was furious at the principal.

He grabbed Earnest, and they left. When they got in the car, Hon explained that he felt the school made a mountain out of a molehill and that it was a just misunderstanding.

Earnest nodded, trying to understand, and asked, "Dad, what's a bra?"

As a parent, you will have countless moments like this one. The teachable moment by the lunch monitor about appropriate humor was lost. We explained to Earnest that what should have happened was that the lunch monitor should have looked in the lunch bag, seen there wasn't anything but lunch, and told the boys that talking about a bra wasn't an appropriate conversation. End of story.

Tip: Being an Advocate

I learned that being an advocate for my boys was critical as they grew up. This didn't mean shouting and banging my fist at teachers, schools, and coaches. I created a few ground rules for myself.

- In the words of Stephen R. Covey, "Seek first to understand, then to be understood."

- Convey that Hon and I were on their "team" when it made sense and look for solutions to the issue and avoid blaming.

- Understand what my boys needed, like recess, and when to push back.

There were several interactions with that elementary school that made us realize we needed to be advocates for our boys. If we didn't do our best to understand what was going on and advocate on their behalf to find a solution, nobody would.

When Earnest was in second grade, he decided that he wasn't going to go to school anymore. Ugh! Earnest explained that he couldn't go outside during recess most days because he hadn't finished his morning work. Anyone who didn't finish had to stay inside during recess and finish. I think recess, lunch, and gym were the only reasons my boys wanted to go to school. Holding him in from recess made him feel punished, dumb, and unmotivated, not to mention that one of the three-legged stool pillars, exercise, was impacted. Recess became one of my non-negotiable school requirements. If you want boys to pay attention during class, you need to let them run around and get the wiggles out.

I scheduled an appointment to talk with the teacher. The three of us worked out a solution to make sure Earnest could enjoy recess and do his schoolwork. We also discussed homework with the teacher. She was shocked to hear that it was taking him over an hour every night to do his homework. We worked together to find a solution for that too.

I remember asking a friend who had seven kids how she dealt with homework. It had become a trying nightly event in our house.

She moaned and said, "Sometimes you need to write with your left hand."

I bust a gut laughing. In my opinion, elementary school homework was there to reinforce what was being taught in the classroom, not supplement the teaching. I pushed back with many teachers on excessive elementary school homework. After Earnest's trying first and second grade, we enrolled the boys in a new school for the next year. I could not imagine how I could make it through that school with Exuberance when I was having so many issues with poor Earnest.

Although the new school had more kids per classroom, it was not an open-space school. Open-space classrooms, an educational brainchild of the sixties, were designed so that there were no walls and doors between classrooms. There were four classrooms in Earnest's second grade, and they all taught in one large space. The teachers had arranged bookcases between the classrooms for privacy, but you could easily hear what was going on in the other classes. Open-space classrooms were not a good match for my boys, who were happy to focus on anything but the teacher when offered a distraction. Switching schools was a very positive experience for both kids.

Math Glasses

Exuberance started at the new school in first grade. At the beginning of second grade, he came home one day and told me that he could not do his math homework anymore because the numbers were spinning. "How about reading?" I ask. "Can you still read?" This issue didn't affect reading, only math. So I read him his math homework out loud.

The next day, his new teacher flagged me down. She told me that Exuberance couldn't do his math because the numbers were spinning. Good grief! OK, time to call Dr. B., the pediatrician. We discussed the possibility of dyslexia, and he recommended starting with a pediatric eye doctor.

At the eye doctor's office, Exuberance seemed to have intermittent problems identifying the letters. The tech put a big eye apparatus in front of him and started spinning the lenses. "Is this better or that?" I'm beginning to feel guilty. Maybe he really does have an eye problem! As we left the room, the doctor pulled me aside and told me that her final test was nothing but glass in the lenses and that his eyes were fine. Phew!

Once out of the office, I explained to Exuberance that he didn't need glasses and that his eyes were perfect. He completely fell apart and cried all the way home. He was so inconsolable that I decided to take him to our local pharmacy to see if I could find fake glasses. I ended up buying the lowest-strength readers I could find, and when we got home, he slapped them on his dilated, bug-eyed eyes, and banged out two math sheets.

Off to school, he went the next day with his dime-store specs and skipped out of the building at the end of the day, exclaiming his math success. Then I really had a dilemma. I couldn't let him keep wearing the dime-store glasses; it might ruin his sight. I spent that weekend looking for cheap fashion glasses. Hon was working on his master's degree, so I dragged both boys from store to store, striking out at each one. After several stores and a last-ditch effort to convince the saleswoman to sell me the discontinued frames, Earnest began to sense something was afoot while Exuberance was spinning happily around the store looking at frames. "Mom," Earnest asks, "does he really *need* glasses?"

"He thinks he does," I answer.

My trip to crazy land was beginning to seem ridiculous even to me, as I was having difficulty finding kid-size fashion glasses. The saleswoman explained that letting a child wear non-shatterproof lenses would be dangerous and that she couldn't sell me a sample frame. I looked at Exuberance, who was trying to wrestle with Earnest. "Good point!" I phoned Hon to discuss my dilemma of spending money on fake glasses. He tells me to stop running around and buy the glasses. It was the best $100 I'd ever spent. I ordered the glasses and amused the saleswoman, who was then considering a new marketing scheme. Exuberance was spinning around the store in excitement, and Earnest was shaking his head and trying hard not to laugh at me.

The glasses arrived, and Exuberance danced off to school with his new math glasses. A week or so later, I checked in with his teacher. She reported a remarkable improvement in math, "Although, today I asked him to get his glasses out for math, and he said he didn't need them. He had in contacts." Pretend contacts! Why didn't I think of that? I could have saved some money!

Exuberance's math glasses in action

So what's the takeaway from this crazy story? Sometimes, you have to trust your heart over your head when sowing confidence in your son. Sister Sense broke it down for me: Exuberance would have preferred to wear a cape but instead figured out a confidence placebo effect, and that the glasses make him look smart, feel smart, be smart. Footnote: I eventually confessed to his teacher that he didn't need glasses, just confidence. She later reported that his math glasses were her favorite barometer for determining if her class understood a lesson. She would be teaching, and Exuberance would suddenly dig into his desk and slap on his glasses. Seeing his smart look, she knew she'd probably just lost half of the class and would recap what she had just taught. Exuberance only wore his math glasses for about a year and discovered other ways to build confidence as he grew older.

Boys Only Book Club

I found that both of my boys were self-conscious and nervous about reading when they were in elementary school, and I have a couple of theories: they did not have the attention span needed to read, they often did not find the stories interesting, or they would rather have been playing.

In an effort to get them excited about reading, I created the Boys Only Book Club around a wonderful series: *The Spiderwick Chronicles*. *Spiderwick* had some elements that were very attractive to third graders:
- The books were small, leather-bound, with short chapters and fabulous artwork.
- They offered an imaginative world featuring fairies, trolls, and goblins that lived all around us.
- There were clever add-on books like the "Field Guide," an Audubon-style book that could be dragged into the yard as they looked for life unseen.

I coordinated with a handful of other boy moms, and we devised an achievable schedule for our sons to read each book to us. After each book, the boys would hold their Boys Only Book Club meeting where we'd gather around the table with popcorn and snacks to discuss the book. I encouraged a heated conversation about the story's fairies and goblins. Each boy had to offer a comment or opinion about the book, and the whole discussion lasted a maximum of twenty minutes. Then popsicles were passed out, the boys ran outside to play, and the MOB enjoyed each other's company.

The boys remembered the fun and associated it with reading. When the movie came out, we all went to the theater together and then had a fun discussion about the difference between movies and books. We compared notes regarding what was left out and how they would have made a better movie.

Making reading into a boy-style event took away the fear that my kids had about reading and introduced them to the imaginative world of books. Making reading fun and optional, not homework, laid the foundation for a lifetime of reading.

Sister Sense - It Doesn't Matter What They Read

I remember being concerned that Earnest and Exuberance only wanted to only read graphic novels. Sister Sense told me it's important to let them choose what they're interested in, so they enjoy reading.

Another suggestion was to turn on the closed captioning of your television. Thank you, Japanese anime, for honing that skill! I'm very impressed how quickly both boys read now.

Professionals and Tutors

Even though we supplied confidence-supporting items like "math glasses," Spiderman backpacks, and new sneakers, both boys needed additional support to supplement what they did not absorb in school, and we could not teach. Rarely did solutions for one child work for the other one. When things were going bad with Earnest, he would spin inward and get reserved and quiet. Exuberance, on the other hand, would spin outward and bounce around like a ball. Teachers had a tendency to notice Exuberance's frustration and energy more than a quiet Earnest. His quiet nature and space cadet tendencies had caused him to fall behind. By third grade, even with a new school, it was obvious that Earnest had fallen behind in some subjects and needed some additional help. We looked at our options and signed him up for a tutoring center. With the additional one-on-one tutoring, his attention in school, confidence, and attitude turned around. Exuberance also went through the tutoring center to keep him up to speed.

An elementary school guidance counselor once told me that girls performed better in elementary school because of maturity and the

> **Tip: The Pushmi-Pullyu**
>
> There was a two-headed llama in Dr. Dolittle's stories called the Pushmi-Pullyu. As a mother, I often felt like a Pushmi-Pullyu, pushing or pulling the boys when they needed help or identifying a solution like a tutor. My big takeaways were:
>
> 1. My boys seem to mature slower than the girls in their classes. Comparing their maturity and success to boys of the same age was a better indicator of when to push and pull. Discussions with the MOB were helpful in those benchmarks.
> 2. The boys were more receptive to tutors when we called them "coach." We had academic coaches, organizational coaches, life coaches (mental), and athletic coaches.

abundance of female teachers. The boys would eventually catch up in middle and high school. That was our experience too.

I think it's important to recognize your own capabilities and strengths and identify when you need help. Finding a tribe of professionals we could trust was critical to raising the boys. At some point, we began calling these support professionals coaches. A coach was much friendlier to the boys than a tutor or child psychologist. We also used high school kids and after-school programs as tutors, which were much more agreeable to the family budget.

> ### Tip: Back-to-School Basics
>
> **Back-to-School Shopping:** All my boys really cared about were new sneakers and a backpack or lunch box with a superhero on it. There was no need to bring them along to the store for anything else.
>
> **Lost and Found:** *Write your last name on everything.* Since Earnest's stuff would be passed down to Exuberance, there was no need to write the first name. Find out where the lost and found is and look every time you go into the school. I was always impressed when I could retrieve items on back-to-school night at the start of the school year.

Lack of Male Teachers

In my experience, males in elementary school tend to be principals, gym teachers, and custodians. There were *very few* male elementary school teachers for our boys. Earnest's first male classroom teacher was in middle school, and Exuberance's first male teacher was in fourth grade.

Exuberance had a particularly trying third-grade year with a teacher who didn't seem to have patience with the wiggly boys in the class. She would turn his desk over and dump the contents on the floor if it was messy and punish him by not allowing him to go outside and play during recess. Hon and I enrolled him in a tutoring program since he did not seem to be keeping up with the class, and I volunteered to be a class mom and read books to the class so that I could get a better idea of what was going on. Exuberance was trying too. I remember him bringing the teacher an apple on Valentine's Day with a note that said she was his favorite teacher. Buttering her up didn't seem to work either. I had already talked to the school guidance counselor, who explained that changing teachers during the school year was not possible and that the principal would not approve it. So Hon and I scheduled a meeting with the teacher and brought in Exuberance's tutor in the hopes that we could find a solution. That meeting didn't result in any progress either. Hon and I encouraged Exuberance to keep his head down and do the best he could until the school year was over. I think that year would have been an educational loss if we hadn't supplemented the learning with the tutoring program.

At the end of the school year, I sat down with the guidance counselor, requested, and then begged that Exuberance be assigned to one of the two male fourth-grade teachers the following year. I felt strongly that he needed a male role model in the school environment. What a difference that made! Exuberance and the other kids in the class were encouraged to wear their favorite sports team's shirt and talk about football games before class started. That year restored his desire to go to school, and I will forever be grateful for that male teacher's enthusiasm, talent, and kindness. I still have a picture from Halloween with the entire class hanging on the jungle gym with the teacher dressed up as an old lady. The kids just loved him.

> **Tip: You Need to Say It Three Times Before They Hear You**
>
> "Shut the door, shut the door, shut the door!"

A-D-H-D versus B-O-Y

I'll be honest, this is another hard nut to crack. When does the nature of a boy, who may not be interested in sitting in a classroom on a beautiful day transition to a learning disability like Attention Deficit Hyperactivity Disorder (ADHD)? This was a question I asked many educational professionals, "Are you sure it's A-D-H-D and not just B-O-Y?" They didn't always appreciate my sense of humor, but it was a real question.

When Earnest was in first or second grade, I sent his elementary school a letter, requesting that they test him for ADHD. Crickets. I was telling one of my sisters-in-law about how I hadn't heard anything from the school, and she asked if I requested an IEP. "What's an IEP?" I asked.

She responded, "An Individualized Education Plan. You need to ask for that." And then she explained the school is required by law to respond.

After some research, I discovered that according to the Department of Education: "Under Section 504, your school district must evaluate a student, at no cost to you, if the district believes or has reason to believe a student has a disability and needs special education and/or related services because of that disability."

I adjusted my letter with stronger language of concern and requested that Earnest be evaluated for an IEP (Individualized Education Plan) and received a prompt response to come into the school and discuss Earnest's issues. Since Hon was out of town on business, I asked a special ed teacher and friend to come with me to the school. The principal, guidance counselor, and his teacher were in the meeting. The principal asked why I brought my friend, and I responded, "When I asked to get him tested, I didn't get a response, but when I sent the second letter and included the term, IEP, I heard back right away. I obviously don't know the correct terms, so she's here to interpret and advise me as an expert." Earnest's teacher choked back a laugh.

Now, Earnest was a very bright boy if he was interested, and a high-quality space cadet when he was not interested. Earnest's biggest issue, which dogged him until college, was organization. The school evaluated him and determined that he had executive functioning disorder. There was no doubt in my mind that he was very disorganized.

We tried lots of different solutions to try to help Earnest. I had to dig through his backpack on a regular basis to help find finished homework that he didn't turn in. Checking on homework being turned in on time became easier as schools modernized and moved to online grade systems that I could regularly check.

Exuberance, on the other hand, was the wiggly, high-energy boy who might be fidgeting with his pencil, the kid behind him, or shouting out an answer when he knew it. He was capable of being organized, and if he liked the teacher, might even do it.

Advocating for the boys and communicating with schools and teachers was a regular occurrence throughout their primary education. I always kept the conversation professional and used language that promoted that we were all on the same team. This is a recurring topic, and I will share more as the boys journey through middle and high school.

Tip: Turning in Homework

I'm not sure why this was such an impossible task, but turning homework in was more of a struggle than doing the homework! Earnest's backpack was typically a mess and getting buy-in from the boy *and* the teacher to find a solution for how to manage assignments was essential. A two-pocketed folder was the answer for elementary school with "TO-DO" on one side and "DONE" on the other. Executive functioning and organization were a continuing topic and a struggle for Earnest through high school, but he finally matured and figured it out. I continued to push him to make it his responsibility, so he owned the organizational process.

Weapons

Some things seem to be hard-wired in the brains of my boys! I was always impressed at the magnetic pull a boy had on a ball, and how they could turn nearly anything into a weapon. It didn't need to be an actual weapon to be treated as one. Sticks, blocks, and rope would all be improvised. Exuberance, however, didn't need anything at all! His two hands would swing around his *pretend* sword with the greatest flare, occasionally getting wounded with imaginary blood. *Blood* was one of his favorite words and was pronounced with extra vowels and maybe with a dramatic fall to the ground. I never knew how to respond to my friends who "would never let their child play with a plastic weapon." I thought, "Who needs a toy? My boys were quite capable of using their fingers or a stick."

I gave up fighting the plastic weapon thing and focused on the respect humans thing: "Don't hit your brother with the stick" and the tried and true "You'll put somebody's eye out." There were times when we had a full arsenal of confiscated treasures on top of the refrigerator in time out. "For every action, there is an equal and opposite reaction."

The other thing in our family was the little boys weren't the only ones who liked weapons; the adult males were great admirers too! When Exuberance was about three, Hon's cousin Robby, a graduate of the United States Naval Academy, came into town for a wedding. He appeared from the guest bedroom in his dress uniform, all decked out with medals and a sword! You would have thought Santa Claus just walked through the door as both boys spun around in excitement. Robby, realizing he had a captive audience, pulled his sword out of its sheath and asked Exuberance if he'd like to hold it. Before Hon and I could react, Exuberance had the sword and started swinging it around in the air above his short little head. Robby and Earnest dropped to the floor, and Hon dove across a table and grabbed the little hands and sword. Apparently, the "Don't hand a small male child a sword" lesson was skipped at the Naval Academy.

I learned, dear members of the MOB, that I had to focus on the big boys when it comes to weapon handling. Hon gave Robby the sword back and had him explain to the boys that a sword wasn't a toy and then demonstrated the proper way to handle a weapon.

In my opinion, gun safety is important to teach even if you don't have a gun in your house. Like everything with raising boys, it took many brief conversations before it took hold in our short person's brain. Our unconventional approach to this was to give my dad, "Pop," a Red-Rider BB Gun for Christmas one year. Pop was just getting his grandfather's sea legs, and the BB gun made him *very* popular. Pop grew up in a hunting family on the Eastern Shore of Maryland and had been around shotguns all his life. He demonstrated and showed the boys gun safety. I found the boys absorbed and listened better if the information wasn't coming from Hon or me. It was a true win-win.

Media Literacy Starts with the First Screen

As a video producer, I was concerned about the impact of television and media literacy early in my parenting journey. Media literacy is the education of information, teaching your children to be discerning consumers when they read, watch, and listen. It's critical these days and not, in my opinion, taught adequately in school.

I tried to keep the screen time to a minimum when the kids were little and tuned to PBS although I nearly lost my mind during the *Barney* and *Teletubby* years. The importance of media literacy really hit me when the movie *Dinosaur* came out. It was the first movie that I had seen for children that took animation to a new level. It was a beautiful Disney animation and incredibly realistic. The scales moved with the dinosaur!

I grew up in the time of the *Flintstones*. No one was under the illusion that Dino lived around the corner. Animation has come a long way during my lifetime, and I was worried that my kids wouldn't know what was real and what wasn't. Now, my challenge was to explain how animation was an artist's imagination and not real.

When we plop our kids in front of the TV to make dinner, we need to remember that they may not be able to differentiate between what is real and what isn't, and with the technological leaps of AI-generated graphics, even the professionals have difficulty judging what's real and artificial. I decided to teach my kids that if it comes through a screen, it is someone else's opinion or imagination. To keep it simple for the kids, we taught them initially that what they saw and heard on television was not reality. I explained how many people are involved in creating a TV show—producers, directors, writers, videographers, lighting engineers, editors, talent, and more. Every one of those people may influence the production and add their spin. For example, a lighting engineer might light an interview dramatically, making the person being interviewed seem distrustful, or an editor may weave different interview clips together to change the meaning of what a person actually said. I decided that the simple message to the boys was none of it was real.

As the boys grew older, we discussed how commercials, news, and programs spun information to meet their objectives. "Who do you think was the audience for that commercial?" and "Who were they talking to?" were common conversation starters. We worked hard to teach them to become educated consumers of information. This will be a continuing thread, and I will elaborate on this topic later as the messages changed as the boys grew up and technology advanced. The key for me was to be an active monitor of what my children watched and heard so that we could discuss it, and even block the channel or website when necessary.

Tip: Media Literacy Resources

The NewseumED, newseumed.org, has some terrific resources on its website to help teach media literacy. Check it out!

New Elementary School

When kids are little, parents have a lot of control over their child's social network. As I mentioned earlier, Hon and I pulled the boys out of their open-space elementary school with the difficult principal after a few years, and they started first and third grades at a local Catholic school. At some point, we realized that if we stayed on our current path, we could be paying for school for more than a decade, and that didn't include college. Sister Sense pointed out that you'd better love your entire community by middle school because your ability to control your kid's environment will diminish as they get older, and typically, the size of the school will grow as they move into regional public middle and high schools.

We decided we could not afford to continue to pay for private elementary school and beyond and searched for a new home. We always checked out the elementary, middle, and high schools when exploring new homes and communities. Were there bikes in front of the schools? Were they all locked up? What did the sports fields and library look like?

Fortunately, we found an incredible neighborhood and community and bought a house that needed a lot of TLC. I knew we'd made a great decision before we had even moved in and were there, cleaning up the place. A woman named Sharman stopped by to say she had stopped the boys while riding their bikes and explained to them that they must not ride in the middle of the street. I thanked her and was happy to know this community was a village that cared and would parent the kids if needed.

In retrospect, we should have moved earlier. Earnest started fifth grade in that community and didn't really get a chance to make good friends and settle in before he was off to middle school in sixth grade. Exuberance, who began third grade at the new home became firmly ensconced in the neighborhood and community.

Buckle Up!

A big thank you to *everyone* who included us in their carpool! Carpools are a hysterical experience because it's as though the boys forget there's an adult chauffeuring them in the car. They cuss, confess to their friends the stupid stuff they have done, and relish in silliness. As a working mom, carpools were the only way to keep the after-school activities schedule manageable. In addition to being thoroughly entertaining, you became a surrogate mom to a pack of boys.

One of my first carpools after our move to the new neighborhood was dropping third-grade boys off at lacrosse practice. They piled out of my car, and I shepherded them to the field with hopes of a quick departure to pick up a few things at the nearby grocery store.

One of the boys, Ferdinand, lay in the grass and looked up at the clouds with no interest in running off to practice with everyone else. I bent down and encouraged him to let me help him get into his pads and gear.

"What do you know about lacrosse?" he quizzed me.

Good grief, I'm getting tested on my lacrosse drop-off capabilities by a third-grader. "Well, my brother was an all-American lacrosse player. I used to play catch with him and have been around lacrosse most of my life."

This answer was not enough for Ferdinand. He was not convinced I knew what I was doing and continued, "So if you had the ball and were running to the crease, where would you shoot?"

"Game on, Ferdinand," I think. "Well, because I'm right-handed, I'd fire it at the upper left corner of the net or bounce it in the dirt in front of the goal."

Ferdinand studied me as he considered my answer. I guess I passed because he put out both hands to let me help him lace up his lacrosse gloves. "You're going to have to stand," I say. "I'm not getting on the ground to do that." Up he popped, finally ready to participate.

All these carpool boys live in my heart to this day, and I hug them as hard as I can when I get to see them. These boys' moms became my new MOB, all committed to helping our boys become independent and successful humans. As the boys' friends changed, more women became part of my MOB tribe. With every town, grade, and sport, my comradery with other mothers grew.

Really?

Communication takes practice, and my boys were often too busy to slow down and try to explain themselves. These miscommunications caused misunderstandings with friends and family. When technology gets introduced, things can really go sideways. As moms, it's important for our survival and our boys' future to give them communication building blocks. "Use your words" only seemed to frustrate my kids. In time, I learned to *stop and listen* in those moments instead of compounding their emotions with talking parameters. Often, I needed to wait them out by allowing them to calm down. After a bit of time, making sure the three-legged stool was sturdy and offering a snack, their words would come. Trying to rationalize with a hungry child is hopeless.

The male brain seems to be wired differently and may need time to comprehend and acknowledge they are having emotions before they can discuss them. In addition to helping them learn to talk, I needed to help my boys understand that communication is a toolbox with many different tools: verbal, physical, and written. Earnest was fond of verbal. He started talking early and didn't clam up until middle school. Exuberance preferred physical communication. He'd prefer to bump into you, stomp his foot, or bang on a table if he was frustrated.

It was important for me to learn how to recognize when the boys needed to talk about something. These times often came when we were in the car or at bedtime. When the boys were in elementary school, I tried to lie in their bed, ask them about their day, and read a book together. Those moments of quiet conversation often revealed difficulties they were having in school with the classwork, trying friendships, or bullying. Hon and I would tag team these nightly check-ins, and often, the boys were more willing to talk with him about an issue than me.

We played a game when they were young called Really, which focused on the inflection of words. Really is a fun way to demonstrate how a written word can have a lot of different meanings when spoken with inflection. For us, it was a contest to see who could come up with an original way to say *really*. One lesson behind Really was that when written, the meaning could be misinterpreted, and communication was sometimes more efficient when spoken instead of written.

Really was also a fun way to get them to tell me more. "How was your day?"

"Fine."

"Really?" Game on!

Teaching the boys to appreciate and understand the pros and cons of different forms of communication paid off as they matured. We've all been misunderstood in a text or email when we write a message in a conversational manner instead of talking. Digital communication has made people detached communicators, and sometimes, messages are *sent* when they should have been spoken. These concepts will meet great resistance if they are introduced for the first time during adolescence when eye rolling is a preferred form of communication.

We also had a dinner conversation game called High/Low. Everyone had to go around the table and talk about the best and the worst things that happened during the day. High/Low put the boys, Hon, and me on equal footing, as good and bad things happen to each of us daily. Those conversations were a critical part of our regular family conversation and often led to discussions about more than the high/low moments.

Big Dog, Little Dog

In the documentary *Raising Cain*, they examine ways other cultures encourage empathy. They show a case study of a school in Japan where the older elementary school boys take the male kindergarteners to the bathroom every day. This is beneficial to both older and younger boys. The younger boys get to watch what they see as a role model and look up to an older child. The older boys learn empathy and responsibility by taking care of someone younger.

When my boys were younger, we often had teenage boy babysitters. These boys were my sons' favorite sitters since they still enjoyed playing boy stuff. Many of the girl babysitters were emulating moms; whereas, the boy sitters were just older boys. These teen boys would show up to babysit in the afternoon in the summer on their skateboard or bicycle, and I'd send the three of them off to have fun and not come back unless it was raining or 4:30 p.m. These poor teens would have to negotiate activities between Earnest and Exuberance—"I want to go fishing!" "No, I want to go to the playground!" Frankly, the older boys stood a much better chance of reaching a compromise than I did. In the end, everyone won. I got to get some work done, the male babysitter was humbled by the challenge of watching other children while rising to hero status, and the boys had a new role model and active afternoon.

Pack Your Patience and Humor—You'll need it

Calls from the health room, teachers, or school administrators were a regular occurrence for me. One of my friends who had two girls the same age recently chuckled and said that she never got calls from the school. "You missed out on all the fun, my dear!" Here are two more elementary school stories about Exuberance.

Exuberance Finds a Cool Rock!

Exuberance was made of air. A skinny, bouncy, energetic, and friendly boy. He noticed everything and spun his way through the school day. Once when he was in fourth grade, I got a "Houston, we have a problem" call from his teacher. "Mrs. Sundius, Exuberance brought something into school today that he said he found at the bus stop. A special rock. The special rock was a marble marijuana pipe."

Yikes! "His bus stop is right next to a trail, and the older kids go back there a lot. He didn't get it from our home!" I tried to explain.

"I understand," said the teacher, "and it was obvious that he didn't know what it was when he showed it to me. But by law, I have to report it to a school administrator, which I did. And we both agreed to destroy it and that it didn't need to go any further."

Phew! "Thank you so much for being understanding." I recognize that his outcome could have gone down very differently and was thankful that sometimes common sense does prevail.

Bus Safety Monitor

Incredibly, Exuberance was chosen to be the safety monitor on his bus in fifth grade. I found this quite amusing until one of my friends told me that there were two younger boys crying at her bus stop because they were afraid of Exuberance. Although it was difficult for me to understand how anyone could be afraid of him, I called the young boys' mom to learn more. We agreed to meet at the playground in our neighborhood with all the boys after homework was completed.

I sat Exuberance down when he got home from school and asked him about the bus. He admitted that the safety monitor power was going to his head.

"The little boys don't stay in their seats!"

"How did you behave when you were their age?" I asked. "I think you owe these little boys an apology, don't you? Did you know they are afraid of you?"

He agreed. When we got to the playground, Exuberance apologized for scaring them, and they apologized for not following the bus rules. They all shook hands and ran off to play. That was it. Time and time again, I marveled at the boys' ability to be done with a matter. It didn't turn into a big drama and was more "I'm sorry. Let's go play." It was rare when a disagreement didn't work out this way.

Exuberance was stripped of his safety monitor badge later that week after leaping like Superman out of the back of the bus during a safety drill. What goes around, comes around.

The Sister Gap and Teaching Young Boys How to Treat Girls

Earnest and Exuberance dressed to crash their cousin's Princess Birthday party.

Since the boys didn't have any females in the house except for our dog, Razel, and me, I identified other families that might fill the gap. Learning how to play and treat girls as friends is critical before releasing young males into the wild when they get older. They need to appreciate, respect, and empathize with women, which only comes with experience.

Cousins were our first stop for sister fun, especially since there were a lot of them! The cousins on Hon's side of the family are still close-knit today and have a chat group called "Just Cuz." We also lived close to several girl-only families. I thought it was important to teach the boys how to be friends with girls, and many of those sister friendships still hold today.

As a family, we were always up for a laugh. Once, the boys were invited to their cousin Em's princess birthday party. We thought it would be funny if they dressed as princesses and surprised Em, so we borrowed princess Halloween costumes from some friends with girls in our neighborhood. When my brother and Em answered the door and saw them, they started howling. The whole party laughed hard, and the boys quickly ditched their costumes to run off and play with their cousin Ry.

How to treat and respect women began when my boys were young and is still ongoing. Since we had a house without sisters, I often filled in the gaps with discussions of how to treat girls and women. This dynamic was familiar to other members of the MOB without daughters. It was important to realize that "they don't know what they don't know" and try to find ways to give them the experiences that they are missing.

I remember my father explaining to my brother when he was little that he couldn't hit me, his sister, under any circumstance. "You may not hit a girl, period! It is not acceptable." My brother cried as he tried to comprehend this critical lesson, and I was appreciative of my father for stating that rule clearly.

Dance in the Rain

Often, the most memorable activities didn't cost a penny. My boys and Razel were dirty dogs. They all loved rolling in the mud and dancing in the rain. We loved looking at the clouds and identifying shapes.

Make a fort! Forts are simple. All you need to do is put a blanket over a table. One of our favorite spots was the table on our back deck. One winter, we were blessed with a ridiculous amount of snow, several feet. Hon shoveled a path to the porch table on the deck, and the boys and Razel played in the snow fort for hours!

We also held a Hurricane Irene party with a few families in our neighborhood. The boys all went outside in their underwear, danced, splashed, and were silly in the rain. Not to be outdone, the MOB put on our raincoats and sang, "Goodbye Irene," instead of "Goodnight Irene," an old song. It still brings a smile to all our faces.

Another memorable activity was having a small bonfire. Hon used to grab a shovel and dig a hole in our backyard. We'd sit out there burning sticks and eating s'mores. The next day, Hon would pull the ashes out of the hole, push the dirt in, and drop the grass back on top.

Occasionally, we decommissioned old American flags when they started to fall apart. Earnest would cut the flag into red-and-white stripes and a blue rectangle with stars. Everyone at the bonfire would get a stripe of the flag. One by one, we dropped our part of the flag into the fire and shared a personal statement of pride about the United States. When we were out of flag pieces to burn, we sang "God Bless America" together.

We've always had silly adventures with the kids. We had a group of friends with kids the same age in our old neighborhood and used to commando decorate each other's houses at Christmas. We'd collect the tackiest and largest Christmas decorations we could find, then gather at dark to sneak the decorations onto someone's yard. It was very entertaining for the commandos, the recipients of the attack, and the neighbors.

Shortly after we moved to a new community, those friends snuck down to our new house in the dead of night on the eve of April Fool's Day and decorated the yard with every holiday item they could find. We woke up to large Valentine's hearts, plastic Santa in the basketball net, the Easter Bunny, and large blow-up characters throughout the yard. We all howled! Our friends really got us, and I found plastic Easter eggs in our gardens for years.

My mom was fantastic at making ordinary things fun. When I was a kid, some days we had peanut butter and jelly sandwiches for lunch, but the best days were when we had a Nicky Hokey. A Nicky Hokey was a term she made up for a peanut butter and jelly sandwich, but it came with a song, "It's Nicky Hokey Time," which I later realized sounded a lot like "It's Howdy Doody Time." Thanks, Mom, for teaching me the magic of silly adventures.

The End of Elementary School

Exuberance inherited the aggressively social traits of my family. In his grade, there was a large pack of boys in our new neighborhood who became his good friends. I called them the Boys of the Spit. We lived near a river, and the boys had found a spit of sand that they would play on for hours, not to be confused with *the pit*, also known by adults as a dry pond. The pit was used for sledding and winter fun, and the spit for summer adventures. The MOB of this boy pack was large, and we actively tag-team-tracked the Boys of the Spit's activities.

Our neighborhood had a fun last day of elementary school tradition where parents gathered at the largest bus stop with popsicles and water balloons to celebrate the end of school. There was a full-fledged parent versus kids' water balloon battle when the kids got off the bus. The year that the Boys of the Spit graduated elementary school, this celebration rose to a new level of chaos.

Exuberance and the Boys of the Spit enjoyed their fifth-grade promotion earlier in the day and arrived at their homes with a plan in place. They all leaped on their bikes and hurried through the neighborhood to beat the bus's arrival. By the time I got there, they had already raided the cooler of water balloons and readied themselves for battle. As the bus pulled up, they began lobbing water balloons into the open bus windows and chasing the bus down the road. As the bus came to a stop, the experienced last-day-of-school kids dashed off, using their lunch boxes and backpacks as shields. Dads began to attack the Boys of the Spit to distract them from the poor kindergarteners who were getting off the bus and were hiding behind their beloved art projects. Total mayhem erupted! It is one of the funniest things I have ever seen. Summer fun had begun!

In many ways, this water balloon attack was the end of a chapter. The Boys of the Spit were heading into middle school and would be at the bottom of the pecking order the next year.

Exuberance and the recently graduated fifth-grade boys prepare for the arrival of the bus on the last day of school.

Our Favorite Boy Books	Our Favorite Boy Movies
When You Give a Pig a Pancake (Earnest's favorite)	*Sandlot*
Blueberries for Sal	*Dinosaur*
Where the Wild Things Are (Exuberance's favorite)	*Peter Pan* (all versions)
Everybody Poops (still cracks them up)	*Monsters Inc.*
Captain Underpants	*Balto*
The Spiderwick Chronicles	*Remember the Titans*
The Dangerous Book for Boys	*The NeverEnding Story*
Diary of a Wombat	*Miracle*
Magic Tree House series	*Secondhand Lions*
Harry Potter series	(Any movie with a dragon, swords, or knights!)
Percy Jackson series	

Middle School

◆◉▶

The greatest teacher failure is.
—Yoda, *The Lust Jedi*

Becoming a Submarine Parent?

As I mentioned in the introduction, I believe I made up the term, *submarine parent*. I knew this was going to be my mode of operation as I was juggling my own business and my family. In my mind, a submarine parent is the opposite of a helicopter parent. We float beneath the surface, giving our children the *illusion* of independence while we fact-check information, ping their location, compare stories with other members of the MOB, and on rare occasions, surface in a full breach and pull them back into compliance. The submarine parenting phase slowly declined through their early twenties until they were launched as emerging, truly independent adults.

As you wrestle with how comfortable you are with spying on your kids, remember that there are other forces—computer games, apps, social media platforms, web browsers, and television shows—whose algorithms and influencers are not wrestling at all. Our children are being fed information *all* the time, suggesting ideas that they might not have thought of on their own. When the boys were younger, I was concerned about how realistic animation had become. Next, the danger was being fed misinformation and harmful, potentially deadly, ideas. I will share additional media literacy experiences from their teen years and my takeaways during this developmental period.

My goal for the boys was to allow them to make mistakes and learn critical life lessons while still living at home, so Hon and I could help put them on a positive path. By the time the boys headed off to college, I was encouraged that the foundation of independence was solid, and they had the confidence to tackle the next chapter of their lives.

My goal for myself was to survive. I was my own worst critic and had to learn to be kinder to myself. Juggling kids, their schedules, homework, a career, a house, marriage, and life was *overwhelming*, especially when the boys were in middle school. I had too many balls in the air and was not the best juggler. For me, this was probably the most difficult stage of parenting because I was trying to keep the kids safe while nurturing their independence. I felt like I was drowning during their middle school days.

In this next section of the book, I share my lessons learned, what worked, and what didn't. In many ways, this period from sixth to twelfth grade is scarier than when they are young, but there is no better feeling than watching your child blossom and grow as they cha-cha to adulthood.

Sister Sense—Befriend the Mother of a Female Classmate

It was critical to be the BFF of the mother of a female classmate if I want to know essential information like picture day, science projects, high school dances, and graduation. Neither boy was good at passing on this type of information.

Another tip from the MOB is to jot down the names of the parent you know as you go from class to class, so you can reach out when inevitably something was forgotten, or clarification is needed.

Middle School: A Bumpy Road

When Earnest was in nursery school, I attended a lecture at the school shortly after the September 11 attack that I never forgot. The school brought in a child psychologist to help us understand how to parent during such a tragedy. He cautioned us about letting the kids hear too much news and to wait to have adult conversations about the attack after the kids went to bed. However, he also said our nursery-school-age kids were too little to really comprehend the catastrophe and that the children you had to keep an eye on were your middle-school-age children. Young teens are old enough and aware enough to understand the tragedy but may not be mature enough to process it emotionally. The child psychologist said, "Show me a pessimistic adult, and I'll show you a child that experienced a tragedy before they could emotionally process it."

That statement always stuck with me and made me extra vigilant when the kids were young teenagers. I also noticed the struggle of young teens as life events like divorce, illness of a parent, or death of a grandparent hit their life, causing them emotional turmoil. It was important to appreciate that the boys and their friends did not have the life experience to navigate these events.

As adults, we need to do a dance between shielding our kids from the information they may be too young to understand and talking with them to help them process tragic life moments. Having an open dialogue with my kids began when they were young. I suggest beginning sensitive conversations and then letting the child talk, so you can listen closely. Their comments will direct you as to how much information they are ready to process. Middle school is a tricky age.

Our middle school was sixth through eighth grade. I think middle school is where puberty goes to explode. Hormones and social maturity come in fits and starts. Puberty primarily happened for my boys in high school. That was when they got pimples, had giant growth spurts, started sprouting facial hair, and pulled away from their momma. But for a majority of girls and many other boys, puberty began in middle school.

My skills of becoming a submarine parent were developed and sharpened during this period. Driving a carpool is an opportunity to uncover a wealth of information about what was going on in their school and sports life.

I spent five years in our local middle school, shepherding Earnest and Exuberance. That period is when I truly forged lifelong friendships with other members of the MOB. We trudged the halls during back-to-school meetings and passed each other on the way to the health room, guidance counselor, and principal's offices. We quietly shared concerns, discussed and strategized over complicated adolescence issues, and laughed our heads off.

Thankfully, Earnest was the first to enter middle school, allowing me to get my sea legs. He was a quiet, shy kid with a few good friends. I remember my mom telling me during that time that some boys might be a little slower in making friends and that it took a bit for my brother, who is now known as aggressively social, to make friends. As long as they had one or two good friends, they would be OK. Hon and I encouraged strong friendships at every opportunity. For one of Earnest's birthdays, we took a pack of his friends to a paintball course. Getting them outside and running around was important for their mental and social balance. We would also encourage Earnest to invite his friends over for a barbecue or make-their-own-pizza night. Boys at that age are always starving, making it easy to entice them with a favorite meal.

Looking back, my trips to school to advocate for the boys began in elementary school and never stopped. The boys needed to know that someone had their back and would help them navigate growing up. By the end of elementary school, Earnest had been diagnosed with ADHD, and we worked with a mental health counselor and Dr. B, our pediatrician, to help him learn strategies to stay focused and succeed in school. He started middle school with a 504 plan to improve his learning outcomes. The plan included recommendations to teachers, such as sitting in the front of the room, and he had an elective course offered by our school system called AVID (Advancement Via Individual Determination) that supported kids in the academic middle. The AVID program helped him learn and apply organizational skills and checked his homework and notebooks. The kids in AVID also went on field trips to colleges as motivation for the future. Exuberance went through the AVID program too. One advantage of the public school system is the diversity of educational programs for the kids, but it doesn't happen organically. I had to get advice from other mothers and professionals, do my own research, and then advocate to make it happen.

Earnest's flavor of ADHD made it difficult to remember classmates' names, causing him to be a bit socially repressed. It took persistence to understand the pain points of my boys because, in my experience, they were not great at communicating their feelings. Earnest eventually shared that he did not feel connected to the students he sat with during lunch, making him lonely and sad. The school had a policy of not allowing the kids to choose where they sat during lunch period; instead, they had assigned seating. I couldn't convince Earnest to put himself out there and try to make friends with his assigned lunchmates. I think lunchtime for him was socially stressful and caused him a lot of anxiety. I made an appointment with the school guidance counselor for the two of us and encouraged Earnest to talk about how devastating the lunch period was to him. The guidance counselor agreed that it was unfair for him since he was a well-behaved student and started attending the beginning of Earnest's lunch period to make sure he was allowed to sit with his friends. This little change had a profound effect on Earnest's attitude toward himself and school, and it would not have happened if I hadn't pushed Earnest to explain his feelings to the school's guidance counselor.

I had plenty of opportunities to interact with the faculty and administration with Exuberance too but for totally different reasons. Social interaction was not Exuberance's issue. Keeping his energy level in check was his challenge. He wanted to be everyone's best friend and the class comedian, which caused his interaction with teachers to be very hot or cold. There was never a middle ground. He was all in or totally out.

One of Hon and my strategies and successes was having an attitude that we wanted to partner with the school. Although there were many trying situations over the years, I never entered with a momma-bear attitude, thinking my cub could do no wrong. I respected their experience and expertise in education and wanted to find solutions to the problems at hand, all while keeping the boys accountable for their own actions. "Seek first to understand, then to be understood" was a motto I had to remind myself of every time I walked through those school doors. I found calm determination to be my greatest tactic to arrive at a solution with educators that was fair and achievable.

> ### Tip: It's Never One Thing: Success of the Weighted Blanket
>
> Sleep is one of the pivotal pillars of the three-legged-stool philosophy and happy, healthy kids. Exuberance would tear around all day and drop like a stone when his head hit the pillow. Earnest struggled to fall asleep, especially as a teenager.
>
> Earnest was great at going to bed without screens and loved reading. He was also very good at worrying and had sensory sensitivity. We tried many things to make sleeping easier: a relax period before bedtime, Melatonin, and finally, a weighted blanket. The extra snug, comfortable blanket made the difference, and a friend even sewed a less conspicuous one for him to take to college as a high school graduation gift.
>
> If you try a weighted blanket, I recommend getting one with a duvet cover. Teenagers are stinky, and the weighted blanket will kill your washing machine.

Technology: Can't Live with It, Can't Live without It

Kids are drawn to communication technology, such as cell phones because most adults in their lives are obsessed with it! I found that, often, if my kids were misbehaving, it was because I wasn't paying attention and was distracted by work or my phone. They were such sponges, mimicking what they saw and heard, and I needed to set a better example and be present when communicating with them.

By second grade, both boys had self-contained electronic games with no access to the internet. Access to these devices was limited to times after homework and play. They did not get access to a cell phone or social media like Facebook until about eighth grade. They understood, under duress, that their technology was mine. I could look at it any time I wanted, and I was going to check it regularly. I recognize that many parents provide their children with cell phones in elementary school now. Today's phones are computers with access to the world. It's a lot of technology to put in the hands of a child. My recommendation is to postpone giving access to a cell phone as long as you can, and when you do, set up all the parent monitoring and protection that you can until they are mature enough to manage it.

The boys did not have laptops when they were in middle school. We had a computer in the kitchen that they could use for homework, and I could help them and keep an eye on it. Some of the first computer activities were typing games. The boys never had a television in their bedrooms until they went off to college and bought their own.

Earnest was typically good with the rules for using the computer. Exuberance, on the other hand, was always pushing the boundaries. One evening, when Exuberance was in middle school, and before he was allowed to have a social media account, Facebook asked me if I wanted to friend a new user. Exuberance created his own account with an altered spelling of our last name from Sundius to Sandius. What! The poor child didn't fully understand how social media worked and that Facebook might offer connections to future friends like his *mom*! He had fifty-plus friends within a day of creating the account! Full stop! The account was promptly closed, followed by punishment, and a new round of media literacy conversations.

We often called Exuberance, "Me Too." As the second born, he did not want to wait the additional two years to get the perks that

Earnest received. Technology is very enticing to our teen boys, and the consequences are much too real. There was no doubt in our house that the technology: cell phones, computers, games, and the internet were mine, and I would monitor it in any way I could and take it away in a heartbeat if warranted. The struggle was real, and I was thankful that I taught them that no meant no when they were young.

> ### Tip: Active Listening
>
> During my career as a video producer, I have interviewed hundreds of people. A technique I learned is called *active listening*. This skill was critical as the boys got older since talking is often not their preferred form of communication. The key to active listening is to ask a thoughtful question and wait for the answer. When they finally began talking, I stayed focused on their face, nodding my head, truly listening while refraining from commenting. If I talked too much, they would stop talking, and the opportunity to communicate closed.

Let's Talk about Sex

Thanks, Oprah, for making me feel guilty for not discussing sex with my kids. One day, I had *Oprah* on, and the show was about how important it was to talk with your kids in elementary school about what love and sex are all about because they were already talking about it with their friends. Ugh! I guess visiting the zoo in springtime and watching the Nature Channel isn't enough. Time to put on my big girl pants.

Earnest had just started middle school, and Exuberance was in fourth grade when I brought the subject up to Hon, who looked at me with panicked eyes. Many middle schools discussed puberty and sex as part of the curriculum, and we wanted to get ahead of it. We agreed I would jump in, and he could fill in the blanks from the male perspective.

After a few days of contemplation, I thought, "I'll start with Exuberance! It will be the introductory talk to warm me up, and then I can expand the topic with Earnest." Earnest and Exuberance had different bus times, and the elementary school started earlier, so we had pre-programmed one-on-one time during his breakfast before school.

I sat down with my coffee as Exuberance ate his breakfast. "I want to talk with you about love and sex," I said, jumping in with two feet. "What do you know about it?" I was very proud of myself for coming up with that question, figuring I could adjust the information as needed.

Exuberance looked at me with wisdom. "I know about rape."

My jaw dropped to the floor, and my poor momma brain went into overdrive! *Good grief! I haven't had enough coffee for this,* I thought as I planned my next statement. I finally said, "Rape? What do you know about rape?"

Exuberance answered, "It's bad. I know it's bad."

"Well, we're in agreement there," I say. "But rape isn't really about sex. It's worse than beating someone up. It is a violent, horrible act where one person forces another person to have sex." I then stumble through an explanation of the mechanics of sex, how babies are made, and why it's important to love someone before you venture into sex. Although Exuberance thought he had all answers and knew what rape was, he had no idea how babies are made.

Thankfully, I was saved by the imminent bus, and we wrapped up the conversation, so he could get out the door. As I watched the bus drive off, I was frightened about what he would share on the way to school. The bus ride was always a source of misinformation and mischief. I quickly called one of my friends who had younger kids on the bus to warn her and apologize. She was a nurse.

"Don't worry," she replied. "I had that conversation with my kids when they were in kindergarten."

You can't have too many nurse friends in your life. They don't scare easily and have the answers before you do.

I did a bit more research before leaping into the sex conversation with Earnest. I found a book that explained sex to adolescent boys and had Hon share it with Earnest. I followed up with Earnest a few days later, and we talked about love, sex, and how to treat women.

When I asked him what he thought about the book and if we should share it with Exuberance. He said, "I think it's weird that it was written by a mother and daughter. Why would they write a book for boys? They're girls!"

Again, I was speechless. I'm not a nurse and tripped through these critical conversations, but Hon and I conveyed the information and our values. Conversations about sex and love were not one-and-done talks and continued in smaller bite-size pieces for many years. My only real advice is to get the conversation started, just like Oprah said. Boys need to understand what it means from their mom too, not just other males. Do not leave it up to pop culture, the internet, and the bus to explain sex and love to your kids. Good luck!

Cussing Guidelines

I like to blame my red hair, but I'm just going to lay it out there. I'm not great at following or creating rules, so I tend to keep it simple. Cussing rules were a bit of a conundrum for me because stuff happens, and words fly out of your mouth. I decided to follow my mom's lead and discouraged using profanity with a few exceptions.

- Cussing is not allowed, and adults will do their best to keep it in check.
- "Shit" is a kitchen word, and only mothers get to use it in the kitchen. The kitchen is where the cook can get burned or cut, which is why cussing is limited to only the cook.
- Kids are not allowed to cuss and will be asked not to whether they belong to me or not.

- Loopholes (there were a few exceptions):
    - When playing the game of hearts, you may call the queen of spades the "old bitch." We play some competitive hearts!
    - To pay tribute to artists, you may cuss if it is in the lyrics of a song. Earnest's favorite song when he was eight was John Hiatt's "Master of Disaster" because he could belt out the line: "Now he's just a mean old bastard when he plays the blues."

> ### Sister Sense—Volunteer If You Can Swing It
>
> No matter what the age, there is great value in volunteering at a school. You get to meet other parents, watch your kid in their peer environment, and the school needs and appreciates the help.

The Rat Face Stage

"Rat face" was one of my least favorite phases. It occurred in middle school when juvenile behavior had a contagious effect on the boy pack, and they would look at adults with what they called a rat face. To double down on this ridiculous look, they made sure to ruin every photo they could with this look where they opened their eyes wide, crinkled up their nose, and bit on their lower lip to look like they had rat teeth.

To truly appreciate the rat face phase, I recommend chaperoning an eighth-grade field trip. There you can observe adolescence in the wild where the girls seem as though they are ready to go off to college, and the boys, who have barely reached puberty, are reacting with a rat face and equivalently immature behavior. There is a special place in heaven for middle school teachers.

> ### Recipe—Easy Egg Drop Soup
>
> Exuberance was so hungry when he came home from school or sports, I taught him to make this simple soup to hold him over until dinner.
>
> **Ingredients**
>
> - Lipton Instant Chicken Noodle Soup mix with extra noodles
> - An egg
> - Optional – frozen or fresh vegetables like peas and carrots
>
> **Directions**
>
> Pour the required water into a small pot and bring it to a boil. If you are adding vegetables, add them with the water. Meanwhile, crack the egg into a small bowl and beat it up with a fork. When the water begins to boil add the soup mix and stir. While stirring quickly, pour the beaten egg in. Cook for another minute and enjoy. If desired, add a little soy sauce.

A Scary Situation with Drugs

When Ernest was a sophomore in high school and Exuberance was in eighth grade, my body retaliated. Initially, I thought I was going through menopause from hell, but it turned out to be a ruptured disc in my neck. The ruptured disc thing took months to figure out, and during that time, I was on a lot of painkillers. I don't think our family would have survived that period without the support of the MOB.

The MOB took me off the carpool schedule, a great idea since I was on painkillers, and kept an eye on the boys and their activities since my submarine parent periscope was foggy. After months of struggling with pain, I finally had surgery, and the ruptured disc was replaced with a new titanium and plastic one. It was an incredibly difficult time for me to be a mother.

I was so out of it that friends would come to check on me while the kids were in school, and I'd have no memory of our time together. I called one MOB friend during that time and told her I found a baking dish with her name written on it. She explained to me she had dropped dinner off the day before and that we talked for an hour. I had no memory of it. Needless to say, that time was a bit blurry for me.

But there was a serious moment that I do remember. I was in the habit of casually looking through the boys' rooms in search of drugs or anything concerning while they were out of the house and at school. About a week after surgery, I found a few pills hidden in Exuberance's room that didn't match up with any of the medications I had. I called Sister Sense and asked what to do. She recommended confronting the issue head-on and advised that there's probably more.

She advised, "He's going to lie to you. He won't want to admit it but keep telling him to 'go get the rest.' And when he finally does, follow him."

When Exuberance came home from school that day, I showed him what I found in his room and asked him what it was. He admitted that he had taken one of the pills and felt so sick that he didn't go to school one day. I told him how concerned I was. He was barely a hundred pounds.

"I know you are smart enough to realize how dangerous that is! I want you to go get any other drugs that you have hidden in this house."

He denied there was anything else, but I kept telling him I didn't believe him, just like Sister Sense advised. He reluctantly led the way to our basement. And although I hadn't been medically cleared to go up and down steps yet, I followed him. He went to a hiding spot and pulled out a gallon Ziploc bag. In it was a marijuana bowl, a lighter, and an Old Spice deodorant container. He unscrewed the deodorant cake and pulled out a small baggie of hash.

"Is that everything?" I asked.

He shook his head yes.

I grabbed the drugs, and we went back upstairs.

"It's not mine," he said.

"I have to lie down. I'm spent. Go to your room, and we'll talk about it when your father gets home."

I was completely empty. I lay on the couch, and my eyes just leaked tears. I was in so much pain. I was overwhelmed as a mom and with life in general.

Exuberance reappeared in the doorway, looking like he'd thought of a new excuse. He stopped in dead stride as I turned to him, quietly crying. He had a look like, "I've broken her this time." He then turned around and went back to his room.

I'm not sure all the words in the world could have had the same impact on him as the look we shared at that moment. It was as though the gravity of it all suddenly hit him.

Now, I'd like to be able to tell you that he never touched drugs again, but I know that's not true. I think the reality of the risk and consequences needs to resonate with them for a meaningful change in behavior, and I believe he appreciated what was at risk for his future and was much more careful.

We took several actions with both boys during this period to try to convey our concern about their having a cavalier attitude toward drugs and its consequences. One thing was to reach out to a family friend who had a son who had gotten caught up with drugs in college and struggled with getting clean. The boys talked with both parents about how their lives had been impacted by their child's addiction. I also reached out to their son, now in his twenties, and explained my concerns and asked him to share his story (a PG version) with the boys. He did, and I do think it made an impact and encouraged the boys to weigh their decisions. The drug issue has only gotten scarier with fentanyl. I encourage you not to delay discussing the effects of drugs and addiction with your kids. The conversation can begin when they are young as you explain the dangers of medication in your home.

> ### Tip: Safety First!
>
> A medicine cabinet might work to hide your drugs from little kids, but as your children get older, it's critical to make sure deadly things are not accessible. Looking back, I wish we had invested in a safe. Instead, I was constantly stashing medicine in odd places with the out-of-sight, out-of-mind philosophy. The best hiding spot I heard was from one member of the MOB that hid her pain medicine in a tampon box. Brilliant!

In Sickness and in Health

As life often dictates, my neck surgery was not the only challenge we had as a family that year. We lost Hon's mom, Grammie, to dementia in January, and my neck surgery was in March. When Hon turned fifty the year before, he made a personal goal to join an eight-man bicycle team, Team Friends, to train and compete in the Race Across America (RAAM). I was supportive of Hon and the team, recognizing that it was a bit of a midlife goal and that regular exercise was essential to his mental health and is one of the pillars of the three-legged stool philosophy.

The RAAM race went from Oceanside, California, to Annapolis, Maryland, traveling over three thousand miles in about a week. I thought it was a bit crazy, truth be told, especially when Hon showed me a documentary where riders literally lost control of their neck from riding so much. And then created all kinds of manmade solutions to hold their head up, so they could continue their ride across the country. One rider's team built a contraption that rose up from the handlebars and had a tennis ball at the top where the rider could rest his chin. Good grief!

I was too focused on my recovery to pay much attention to Hon's never-ending training schedule, but about three months after my surgery, race day arrived. I flew to California to support the start of the race and was able to stay with a dear friend who lived in the area. We watched team after team leave the starting line with awe and disbelief.

The next day was Father's Day. My friend and I were happily celebrating with a pedicure and happy hour when I received a call to let me know that Hon had been in a serious bike crash and was in the trauma center in Flagstaff, Arizona. With no direct flights to Flagstaff, my friend and her daughter drove me through the night to reach Hon. Hon's helmet saved his life. He broke nine ribs, several in two places, his collarbone, and had ridiculous road rash, but he was going to be all right.

It was an emotional couple of days. The love and support we received from our families and friends were overwhelming. One friend suddenly appeared in Hon's hospital room one day. I still get emotional, thinking about how incredible it was to see a friend in a moment like that. Everyone had been following Team Friends on Facebook and tracking the team online. Our families stepped in to take care of the boys, who were at home and still in school, to ensure they were cared for and distracted while we managed the injury.

After four days in the hospital, I rented a car and drove Hon to Phoenix to fly home. Since his clothes and personal items were in the team RAAM follow van, puttering across the country at twenty miles per hour, I went shopping for new clothes for him at Walmart. To entertain myself, I purchased him a motorcycle durag[6] with a skeleton motif for his head, a stylish Hawaiian shirt, shorts, and flip-flops to go with his face, arms, and legs that were covered in road rash. Incredibly, our flight arrived back in Maryland in time to join Team Friends in Annapolis. The boys, our family, and friends all

---

[6] A durag is the name of the bandana or cloth tied to the top of someone's hair.

converged in the middle of the night for the celebration as the team crossed the finish line.

So what are my takeaways from that crazy period? I slow-rolled the information to the kids and waited until we knew the facts. I never lied to them and made sure they could ask whatever questions they had, but there was no reason to concern them until I understood what was happening. Social media and communication outside of a small group of people were shut down until I was confident that Hon would recover from his wounds.

Having a community, a village, that we could rely on was critical to surviving that year. It took me two years to fully recover from my neck surgery and a year for Hon to recover from "crash day." People wanted to help, we needed help, and most importantly, I needed to let them help. As a mom, I often would have the "I'm good" attitude and try to be Superwoman. The MOB and Sister Sense dismissed that kind of talk and forced me to accept help. Letting people help in times of trouble is part of being in a community. I had to forgive myself, as many things fell through the cracks, especially with work and the thank-you notes. I often did not remember who supported us with acts of kindness as I was still healing too. Since I was not always able to say thank you, I have tried to pay it forward with phone calls, chicken pot pie dinners, and love and support whenever I hear of a friend in need.

I believe there are invisible threads between family and friends. Currents that hit you in moments of quiet when you are driving down the road or taking a shower make you muse, "Hey, I wonder how so-and-so is doing?" I try to pick up the phone and say hello when I am hit with those thoughts, and often the voice on the other end says, "I can't believe you called me! I was just thinking about you." And as it turns out, we both needed that moment of friendship.

Hon's road rash healed slowly into what the doctor called "traumatic tattoos." Today you can still see his traumatic tattoos caused by the asphalt and gravel in the road, which look like black-and-gray lines on his healed skin. I now think of many life bumps as traumatic tattoos. They're not all visible but are tattooed on your soul.

My final suggestion and lesson learned is that when your spouse is turning fifty and says he wants to buy a new sports car, encourage the idea. In the long run, it's a better solution to a midlife crisis than riding a bicycle across the country.

> ### Tip: Wound Care 2.0
>
> As the boys got older, I taught them to care for their own wounds. Here are some of our basics:
>
> - Clean all wounds with peroxide. Apply antibiotic ointment and cover with a Band-Aid. Since we lived near the Chesapeake Bay where crazy bacteria in the rivers and bay water were common, they needed to be on the lookout for preventing and recognizing infections. We literally had a bottle of peroxide in the shower so that they could pour a little on scrapes after bathing. Waterproof Band-Aids were also on hand because it was impossible to keep them out of the river during hot weather.
> - Tick check! They eventually got in the habit of checking their body for ticks after playing in the woods. Dr. B. advised them to put on antibiotic ointment after we removed a tick to prevent Lyme disease and other tick illnesses.
> - We also kept a small container of Dawn dish soap in their shower. Washing their skin with Dawn after playing in the woods kept them from breaking out from poison ivy.

Soul Putty

Learning to be a mother is full of ups and downs. Balance is not easy. I turned forty when the boys were five and three. I'll be honest; I was exhausted. Razel was a puppy too, and I remember thinking, "Stop looking at me!" Everyone wanted something between the boys,

Razel, and Hon, my cup was empty. Hon gave me a special birthday present that year. He knew how much I loved to play the guitar, and it seemed impossible with little kids. I had always wanted a twelve-string guitar, and he let me pick out a beautiful used Taylor. That guitar helped me reclaim a piece of myself, and I met some great guys who let me jam with them, Bob's Basement Band. We just played for fun, beer, and each other's parties.

I call music my *soul putty*. It helped fill the cracks in my soul made by life. Those cracks are unavoidable; the trick is to find your own soul putty, so you can be there for your kids and soul mate. In my mind, soul putty is something you can do by yourself. It's an activity that allows your mind to relax and recharge, such as a hike or run, reading, yoga, meditation, knitting, or refinishing furniture.

Momma self-care is essential to a happy home. For some odd reason, moms often feel guilty when we take a step back and do something kind for ourselves. I'm here to tell you it is essential to find your soul putty and help your children find theirs.

Playing the guitar wasn't my only soul putty. I also got great comfort from taking a walk and Girls' Night Out and would text out to my friends, "Time for GNO!" Laughing and commiserating with other moms and girlfriends was rejuvenating for me, and it was beneficial to let the house reins drop and get Hon to take over. Those boys' nights were also critical relationship-building blocks for all the males in my house.

I worked hard to help the boys find their soul putty too and encouraged both boys to play the guitar or any instrument. We got them lessons because it's hard to let your mom teach you. Although we've discussed this many times in our house, I do not think playing computer games is soul putty. Sorry, boys!

Running and playing outside was critical to Exuberance's mental and physical well-being. The Boys of the Spit were always throwing a ball, playing games, wrestling, and tearing around on their bikes. They gave the MOB a run for our money, trying to keep track of their activities! Exuberance became a great guitar player. He tinkered with the guitar through middle and high school and leaped in with both feet during college. Playing music became a critical piece of his mental health when he was in college during the COVID-19 pandemic. YouTube and the internet are extraordinary resources for teaching! Exuberance learned to play songs through video demonstrations and accessed the lyrics and chords from websites and apps.

While Earnest loves music too, his soul putty is laughing. He loves reading funny books and graphic novels, listening to podcasts and comedians, and watching movies. Earnest read the entire four-volume set of *The Complete Calvin and Hobbes* in middle school. He would come home after a hard day at school and flip through those books, belly laughing. He also loved building Lego Mindstorm robots and putting together a model or a puzzle. Mindstorm is a super cool introductory robotics platform that includes construction, design, and programming to make robots walk and react. Some middle schools have teams where club members build Mindstorm robots and compete with other schools. These soul putty activities became lifelines during the COVID-19 pandemic and were critical to supporting both boys' mental health.

It's not always obvious what your and your child's soul putty is, but I think it's important to appreciate that it is a critical ingredient of life balance. It's also fun to talk about it with the kids so that they understand what they can do to help themselves feel better. I guess soul putty is like self-soothing for big kids and adults.

Tip: A Singular Moment

Somewhere along the way, Hon and I created a family budget loophole called "a singular moment." A singular moment was an event that didn't occur very often, and we knew that if we didn't find a way to attend the event, we would regret it. At those times, we agreed to close our eyes and take out our credit cards to participate in the not-to-be-missed moment. Out-of-town family weddings are an example of a singular moment. I think one of the successes of our marriage and parenting style was to make room for life's exceptions and not miss celebrating important events and milestones.

Choose the Kid

As your kids get older, you will inevitably become entangled in other people's families. Your child will be friends with a kid, and then you become friends with the mom as you schedule playdates, and boom, the families become friends. I loved that part of being a mom and made some incredible friends in the process.

What is also inevitable is that some of those marriages don't last, and you'll find yourself involved in the repercussions. It's messy, and I have two pieces of advice for these moments: appreciate that you don't know what's going on in someone else's house and choose the kid. The parents will push you to choose a side, and for me, the side to select was the child.

For example, when Exuberance was in third grade, he had a good friend whose parents were divorcing, which meant two birthday parties for the birthday boy. And yes, it was a competition. Exuberance happily went to both. Mom's party was a typical boy's birthday party at home with all the food, cake, and craziness in action. Dad's party was interesting. The dad had us drop the kids off in the parking lot of a local shopping center. He loaded the boys into his vehicle and said they were off to play laser tag, which sounded like a great boy day. A parking lot pickup time was identified, and off they went. When I picked up Exuberance, he had on a new T-shirt that showcased a ripped style at the armholes and collar. He leaped happily into the car with a big grin on his face. "It looks like you had a great time. Where'd you get that shirt?" I asked.

He happily told me everything they did, then pronounced, "We went to Hoots!"

"Hoots?" I replied, "You went where? Were the waitresses dressed in short orange shorts?"

"Yes!" he answered enthusiastically. "It was great! They have the best wings ever!"

Steam escaped from my ears as I second-guessed my trust in the dad-planned birthday party. I didn't say too much the rest of the drive home, as I thought about how I felt about Hoots. When Hon returned from work that evening, I shared the details of the Hoots birthday party and how I felt it was an inappropriate location for nine-year-olds and asked him to go to Exuberance's room and talk with him about it. By that time, Exuberance had taken off his shirt, found some straight pins, and pinned the shirt to the wall above his bed. He was excited to tell Hon all about the birthday party.

Hon listened, then asked, "Do you know why your mom is not happy about you going to Hoots?"

Exuberance shook his head no.

Hon then explained that I did not appreciate the sexy uniforms required for the waitresses to wear. Hon looked at the shirt now hanging on the bedroom wall. "Do you want to have a good relationship with your mom? If so, I suggest you take the Hoots T-shirt down."

Exuberance took the shirt off his wall.

Although I was not happy with the Hoots party, it was not the last birthday he attended for that kid hosted by his dad. I learned to ask a lot more questions since I had no trust in his knucklehead judgment. Still, I also knew how important it was to support Exuberance's friend as he navigated living in two homes, and I did not regret letting Exuberance go. Hon helped express my expectations of how women should be treated; the experience did not harm Exuberance, and it meant the world to his friend.

Although our house was often a mess, I believe it was a haven for several struggling friends of the boys over the years, a home away from home. As moms, we sometimes fill in the love and parenting gaps of other children, just as the MOB did for me when I was going through my neck surgery. I was always clear about what our house rules were and found the kids appreciated knowing the boundaries. In our neighborhood, the closest mom got to parent the child and passed out hugs, and I was happy to do my part.

Parenting Balance

Parenting a teen is tricky! They are hormonal crazy people. Teens behave one moment like they are ready to head off to make their fortune, and the next minute, they act like a two-year-old having a meltdown. Those of us who are not going through puberty do not have to feed the crazy or join in that behavior. We can act like the adults in the room and help calm and guide our children and their friends toward a positive future.

Parenting is kind of like learning to drive a manual car. If you've never had the pleasure, let me explain the art of the gas, clutch, and stick shift. The gas and clutch are pushed in and released in opposite directions. If you push the clutch down with one foot, you need to ease up on the gas with the other. When you get this dance wrong, the car revolts and stalls or jumps forward. To shift to a higher gear, the driver needs to push the clutch all the way down while taking their foot off the gas, then shift to the next gear. Once in the next gear, one foot backs off the clutch while the other increases the gas. There is an interactive, four-limb balance to driving a manual car.

When my boys were teenagers, my parenting style had to adjust from coasting (clutch) to giddyup (gas) with adaptable guidance. There were plenty of stalls, lurches forward, and grinding gears as I tried to adapt to their hormonal ups and downs. Hon and I found our input was most successful when we could keep the boys moving in the right direction and tap on the brakes instead of slamming them, offering them small course corrections instead of wrenching the wheel. Just like finding the clutch balance, I encourage you to find your parenting balance as you learn to adapt to the ever-changing needs of your child.

> **Tip: Socks and Spoons**
>
> I truly have no explanation for the disappearance of a single sock or the loss of spoons from my flatware. I always suspected the spoons were just tossed in the garbage can by clueless boys.
>
> When the boys were little, I'd pay them ten cents for every pair of socks they matched. By the time they got to middle school and were doing their own laundry, I gave up on solving the sock mystery. One of the great surprises of the universe is when your dryer suddenly coughs up a toddler sock a decade after you've had a person that size in your house.

Cider Misunderstanding

Exuberance had many friends and fully inherited the aggressive social traits of my family. I always found it interesting that he would shift from friend group to friend group based on his energy level. He was primarily in a high-energy pack, running around the neighborhood. But he also had friends who were gamers, and especially on days when he was tired, he'd hang out with his buddies, playing video games.

He was about thirteen and with one of those buddies when he was invited to join him on an overnight game-a-thon at another friend's house. I called the MOB member I knew and discussed logistics. We were both excited about the possibility of a date night ever since we were on reduced mommy duty. I agreed to drop off the boys, and she'd pick up the boys the next day. She explained that she had known the woman whose house I was dropping them off at for many years. The woman was a single mom and a little OCD, which is typically a good quality in a member of the MOB.

I drove the boys to the house, delivered them to the door, and introduced myself to the mom. She invited me in, and we chatted in her kitchen. She explained in excessive detail her concerns with the tap water in her town and how she only used bottled water. I quickly identified her as a safety mom, and I knew it's always good to have one of those around.

I called down the stairs to the gaming boys and asked Exuberance to come up to say goodbye. He bounded up the stairs with a bottle in his hand.

"Mom, you have to taste this! It's the best cider I've ever had," he exclaimed.

I grabbed the bottle and tasted it, then looked at the label. It was hard cider with an alcohol level of over 5 percent. I looked at the other mother, "Do you realize that this is alcohol?"

She looked back with shock and explained that her son had accidentally grabbed it at the grocery store. I anxiously accepted her explanation, gave Exuberance a hug, and reminded him to *think* and call me if he needed anything. When I got to the car, I called my MOB friend, told her about the hard cider, and said, "I'm trying hard to process how she can be concerned about the tap water and oblivious about hard cider. Should I go back in there and get them?" My friend assured me the boys were safe, and the other mom was just a bit ditzy. I decided to trust my friend's judgment and Exuberance's common sense since he knew something was up with that cider and gave it to me to taste.

Highly Mediocre Parenting

As my boys' time in elementary school came to a close, I realized that motherhood perfection was unrealistic, and my new goal was to be highly mediocre. My thought was that as a highly mediocre parent, I could be a little kinder to myself as I strove for a more realistic goal, encourage independence in the boys, and dismiss comments from the kids like, "My friend so-and-so's mom let him (insert activity or new tech toy here)."

I would respond, "Well, she's obviously a better mother than I am." The bar is lower as a highly mediocre parent, so you can focus on the important stuff and not lose energy on noncritical issues. Since the boys did not get cell phones until about eighth grade, I kept track of them the old-fashioned way. They had to tell me where they were going and when they would be back, then I confirmed their location with the MOB.

When it was time for the boys to get cell phones, I had no interest in buying an expensive phone for someone who couldn't remember where their bookbag was half the time and was quite capable of jumping in the water, breaking, or losing a cell phone. My solution was to purchase a SIM card from my cell provider and put it in a phone of the boy's choosing that they bought with their own money. I pulled the SIM card out of the phone they purchased and popped in the SIM card attached to my cell plan. Needless to say, the phones they purchased were not super expensive.

The other benefit of a cheaper cell phone was they had less functionality. They couldn't fill them with games and apps, and it removed them from the competitive rat race of keeping up with the Joneses. If they wanted something badly enough, they could work, save their money, and buy it themselves.

I recognize having your child buy their own cell phone might seem like cruel and unusual punishment to some people, and if you ask a tween, a cell phone is a rite of passage. In my opinion, smartphones can be dangerous technology for an immature brain, and making them save their money to buy it themselves offered two really positive benefits: first, because they had to work and save to purchase it, they took better care of it; second, it delayed them getting a phone. We weren't saying, "No, you can't have a phone"; we were saying, "You have to buy it with your own money, then I will pay the monthly fee for it on our cell phone plan."

Don't Bite

I have come to realize that not all communication is good. Sometimes people just want to bait you into an argument. I imagine myself as the fish and the other person fly fishing, flicking comments at me, and trying to get me into an argument. Ping, ping, ping as the bait bounces on the water, trying to get me to bite. I try to be picky about when I choose to argue with someone, especially my children.

With the boys, the actual issue at hand often had nothing to do with the argument they were trying to pull me into, and it took some time to uncover the real problem. I had the best luck at having a meaningful discussion if I could get them by themselves in a quiet location. The car was always a winning opportunity to talk because they were often in the back seat and didn't have to look at me during the conversation. A closed environment like a car also makes it easier to listen.

Don't forget the important hunger leg of the three-legged stool!" Growing boys are *always* hungry, and often, the barbs that may be coming your way are because they don't realize they need a snack. A quick visit to an ice cream or frozen yogurt shop where we could sit down and chat was often productive, and it helped promote a meaningful conversation rather than an argument.

I'm sure you can relate to the most volatile time of the day in our household, the moments *just* before dinner. Hon would walk in from work, and there were three hungry males in the house. Having a quick appetizer at the ready, particularly if things heat up before you finish cooking, was critical. Any member of the MOB can tell you that a long work/school/sports day plus adolescent male(s) plus hunger before dinner is tricky. Keep conversations light and wait until the end of dinner when bellies are full to discuss anything serious.

Buffalo Chicken Soup

I loved when the Boys of the Spit would hang out at the house. Making this soup was one of the bribes that would get them to appear. It is a boy favorite!

Ingredients

- 2 tablespoon butter
- 1 medium onion chopped
- Heart of celery and 2–3 stalks chopped (I always make soup and stew with the heart. Peel off the bigger stalks; cut the very top and bottom off, then chop up the leaves and remaining stalks.)
- 2–3 medium carrots peeled and chopped small
- 1 tablespoon flour
- 1 packet ranch seasoning (optional)
- 3 quarts chicken stock
- 1/4 cup buffalo wing sauce (or more to taste)
- Rotisserie chicken from the grocery store (remove bones, skin and chop)
- 8 ounces of cream cheese or 2 cups of cream or milk
- Salt and pepper to taste
- Garnish (optional): crumbled blue cheese

Instructions

- Take the cream cheese out of the fridge and let it soften up prior to starting the recipe or microwave it for twenty to thirty seconds if you forget.
- Add the butter to a pot over medium-high heat. Sauté the onions, celery, and carrots until soft.
- Stir in the flour and ranch seasoning, followed by the chicken stock and wing sauce.
- Add chopped chicken, reduce heat to medium.
- Add the cream cheese or cream to the soup. Mix it while it melts.
- Season the soup with salt and pepper and more hot sauce to taste. Garnish with blue cheese.

When in Doubt, Phone the Sister Gap Network for Clarification

The funny thing about being the sole female in your house is that the moments of total male confusion sneak up on you when you least expect it. Understanding what a girl was trying to tell them was a regular mystery for the boys. We didn't put any rules in place when it came to dating except that we weren't paying for dating activities, and a girlfriend might expect the boys to part with their beloved money. Not paying for dates was another benefit of being a highly mediocre parent. Both boys didn't really date until high school and were ready to spend some of their hard-earned cash.

One day, Earnest came home from school and asked for help decoding a conversation he had with a girl. "She said she like liked me. What's the difference between like and like like?"

I offered, "I guess she really likes you!"

Earnest was not fooled. He knew my middle school slang was rusty. It was time to phone a cousin. We called my sister-in-law who had three girls about the same age. The female tribe of cousins and aunts offered many suggestions to Earnest. There were lots of giggles, and when they set him straight, he was ready to brave middle school society again.

Our boys were a resource for some of the girl cousins too, as they were brotherless and needed advice navigating the world of boys. When the boys were younger, we were fortunate to be good friends with families with girls the same age as our boys. Now that Earnest and Exuberance were older, female cousins stepped in to fill the important sister gap.

Brother Fighting Peaks

Sibling fighting is inevitable. In our house, there was little doubt that a confrontation was underway because it was loud. They had skirmishes throughout their life that would include screaming, shouting, slamming doors, wrestling, hitting, throwing things, and on occasion, crying. The worst of those years was when they were both in middle school, Earnest in eighth grade and Exuberance in sixth. I had started a new job the year before, and three days a week, they were on their own for about thirty minutes after school.

Earnest was taking an ADHD medication at that time, which would wear off around the time he got off the bus. All he wanted to do was be quiet in his room. Exuberance, on the other hand, was bouncing off the walls like looney tunes because he had been still and "behaved" all day.

When I was home, I could shore up the three-legged stool with a snack and send Exuberance outside to run around. Left to manage on their own, mayhem erupted. Exuberance would bug Earnest until a fight broke out, which typically coincided with the time I walked through the door from work.

The ringtone on my cell phone for the house was the Beatles' "Help." My coworkers were toughly entertained when my cell broadcast, "(Help) I need somebody, (Help) not just anybody, (Help) you know I need someone, help!" It seemed ridiculous that they couldn't manage thirty minutes without wanting to kill each other, but that was the current state of their maturity. I had the give job and wasn't making enough money for it to be worth the mayhem to our family, so I adapted my work schedule and went back to working freelance.

Around that time, I went on a post-dinner kitchen strike and refused to clean the dishes if I made the dinner. Hon jumped on the bandwagon and insisted that the boys clean the kitchen. Every night after dinner, great negotiations would occur as the boys decided whose turn it was to clean up. My attitude was, "Figure it out." I didn't care if they did it together or alternated nights, but I was not going to referee or manage it. "Figure it out, boys." Hon had less patience for bickering and wanted to do quality control. With effort, I convinced him to ignore them and watch the news with me.

We didn't realize it at the time but forcing them to be responsible for the dishes each night and figuring out how to work together was an important part of developing and improving their relationship. Although the kitchen still needed a bit of cleanup when they were done, it improved over time and taught them basic life skills. I dream that someday a spouse will thank me, and the boys' self-sufficiency will be appreciated.

I remember the boys giggling a few years later as Exuberance was coaching a girlfriend over the phone on how to stack and start the dishwasher. Her parents had gone out of town, and she was using paper plates because she didn't know how to operate the dishwasher. After getting off the phone, the boys howled with laughter.

"Can you believe it! She doesn't know how to do the dishes," Earnest exclaimed, having overheard the conversation.

"She obviously doesn't have a highly mediocre parent," I pronounced and joined in the laughter.

SEP: Somebody Else's Problem

Douglas Adam is one of my favorite satirists. In his book *Life, the Universe, and Everything*, he describes a futuristic spaceship with a SEP field, the ship's new cloaking device. According to one of the main characters, "An SEP is something we can't see, or don't see, or our brain doesn't let us see, because we think that it's "Somebody Else's Problem."

Middle school came with a lot of drama, and I tried to teach the boys how to navigate the emotional ups and downs. I adapted this funny term to teach the boys when *not* to get involved in someone else's problem, a SEP. It's important to recognize a SEP, and you can be empathetic to the person with the problem but be selective in what you make your problem.

I also shared the *don't bite* philosophy, which I used myself to manage conflicts with them. Here I encouraged them to avoid being baited into conflicts with other kids. Exuberance, in particular, always had the energy to jump into the crazy, and I encouraged him for years to be selective.

The Family That Laughs Together Stays Together

Fontrum[7] is a *sniglet*, a made-up word to describe something that doesn't exist in the dictionary. My family made it up or adopted it when I was in college in the 1980s. The family definition is "the wincing feeling you get in the pit of your stomach as you watch someone unbeknown to them make an ass of him- or herself." According to our rules, fontrum is felt by others watching the action and not the individual performing the action. The perpetrator can experience retrospective fontrum after the act in a moment of self-awareness and shame.

I did not grow up in a large family, so we'd get together with my mom's sister's family for Christmas or Thanksgiving. My brother and I had three cousins, and we were all within five years of each other. There was a point during my high school childhood when the adults were upstairs, and the kids hung out in the basement during the holiday pilgrimages.

Something shifted when we were in college, and the two families began a tradition of competitive storytelling at the end of dinner. Winners were crowned based on applause and laughter. Fontrum was one of the main awards categories. Someone would stand and nominate another family member for fontrum then launch into a story of why they were embarrassed for the person, elaborating on their outstanding performance. There were always shouts of astonishment and horror, and the competition was fierce. Over the years, I developed some critical strategies; the most important was never to defend yourself but rather spin the wheel of misfortune with a new story about someone else. When you defended yourself, you only prolonged the pain and relived your fontrum experience as the family critics started asking piercing questions that could never be fully explained. The best course of action was to agree that it was fontrum, then spin the wheel to someone else and hope they defend themselves.

---

[7] Fontrum: A made-up word that describes the wincing feeling you get in the pit of your stomach as you watch someone, unbeknown to themselves, make a fool of themselves. By definition, you can only have it for yourself in retrospect.

Here's a classic story as told by the king of storytelling, my bro, to illustrate how fontrum and the yearly awards worked. He nominated my younger female cousin, J. A. Nice.

As his story goes, "J. A. Nice and I were invited to a wedding in San Francisco, one of the first post-college weddings we attended. Since there were only a few of us who flew in for the big day, the bride and groom invited us back to their wedding suite after the reception. We were hanging out, having a drink, and watching *Saturday Night Live*. As things began to quiet down, I looked around to see where the bride and groom were. I was horrified to discover that J. A. Nice was asleep in the center of the king bed with the bride and groom on either side."

Laughter and "No!" erupted from the dinner table. My aunt shouted, "You didn't!"

J. A. Nice, making a crucial error by attempting to defend herself instead of spinning the wheel, exclaimed, "But I was there first!" And we all had fontrum for her again.

Back then, when you won fontrum, you had to have your picture taken with a paper bag over your head because we were so embarrassed to be with you. Now you might think this is all ridiculous, but there were several therapeutic benefits. We learned to tell fontrum stories about ourselves as we moved away and no longer lived close to each other. The funny thing was that you would share your most embarrassing moment of the year, the event that you were sure was award-winning fontrum, and it would be brushed aside as not worthy. The family's ability to share and laugh at ourselves was healing, and when our kids were teens, it was time to teach this self-deprecating trait to the next generation.

The question for the family then was how to add some new age-appropriate PG laughter into our yearly holiday competitions. We felt that family silliness was an important part of our family unity. The family that laughs together stays together. There were seven kids separated by only five years in this new generation of my boys, nieces, and nephews. A new family competition was created: competitive lip-syncing. Contestants submitted a one-minute recording of lip-syncing on video by the time the appetizers were served. The videos are shown to the entire family and judged by a nonfamily member attendee. The judge always mentioned something he appreciated about each video as he scored the videos and announced the winner.

Typically, the videos were created earlier that day as we were not great planners. Costumes were worn, people cross-dressed, there was choreography, and the music ranged from classic rock to hip-hop. One year, we submitted an incredible family lip-syncing performance of Queen's "Bohemian Rhapsody" planned during the thirty-minute car ride to Bro's house. Another year, we recorded Mariah Carey's "All I Want For Christmas Is You" during the car ride with two well-positioned iPhones, so we didn't miss the backseat performers. Inconceivably, we never won! The competition was stiff, as everyone wanted bragging rights.

I share these silly family escapades because they have been such successful family bonding experiences over multiple generations for over forty years. Laughter is not only good medicine; it can bond generations.

Family lip-syncing competition. The competition was fierce.

The Frightening and Endearing Man-Cub

You'll know a man-cub[8] when you see one. They are fast-growing males with arms and legs like tree trunks. Man-cubs are known for misjudging the width of a doorway and bouncing off it as they enter a room. It's like they do not understand where their arms end as their hands make fingerprint lines down your hallway walls. Man-cubs also look like they are wearing clown shoes to accommodate their quickly growing feet.

The frightening and sometimes endearing thing about the man-cub is that their common sense and ability to make good decisions is in hibernation. The testosterone that causes the pimples to sprout and limbs to grow also makes them silly, immature, and foolhardy. In my experience, there is approximately a six-year window for the man-cub phase, as kids enter puberty at many different ages. Earnest's man-cub growth spurt happened gradually, beginning in middle school and winding down at the end of high school. Exuberance's man-cub phase progressed slowly until his junior year of high school when he suddenly grew six inches in a year. In middle school, he was so skinny that his goal was to get the passenger seat airbag light to turn off. He would bounce up and down in the seat, trying to prove that he was big enough to sit shotgun.

Man-cubs can also be reckless. Their sense of "this might not be a good idea" is dulled by hormones, and when combined with a tribe of friends trying to outdo each other, the results can be frightening. They often walked the neighborhood together in a little pack, and their dangerous antics only grew as they got taller and began high school. As a submarine parent, I wanted the energetic man-cubs to feel like meerkats on top of their hill, looking around on high alert if they were up to no good, and fearing that a member of the MOB would swoop in like a hawk at any moment to quash their crazy ideas.

---

[8] Man-cub: A nickname for young males who are large in size and still incredibly immature.

Smells Like Teen Spirit

There will be no doubt that your cute little boy has become a man-cub. Your nose will alert you to this transformation. One day, you are driving a giggly pack of boys to sports, and then next, you are diving for the window-down button in your car, thinking, "Holy cow! They stink!" And it gets worse because the self-aware boys will start dousing themselves in Ax or Irish Spring. Survival tip: *Roll the windows down!* They won't notice, and your eyes will stop watering, so you can drive safely. Remember, the chauffeur can learn a lot by closing her mouth and opening her ears during carpool sessions. Their language can get a bit spicy as they try to outdo each other, but the intelligence collecting is worth staying quiet.

Stinky laundry was a momma out[9] point for me, and I taught the boys how to do their own laundry. It was a simple lesson because everything needed to be washed on *hot*. Separating clothes by color and cold versus warm water laundry is an advanced class saved for high school seniors. And don't let them forget those sports pads and uniforms. After all, bacteria are having a party in their sports gear. Exuberance used to get staph infections that looked like pimples on his elbows and the back of his knees because of less-than-clean sports gear. The pimple-like infections needed to be treated with peroxide, antibiotic ointment, and momma's watchful eye to avoid becoming something more serious. Some people hypothesize that the staph infections came from the field or turf, but all you need to do is smell the dirty dogs' stinky sports gear to know where it originated. Sister Sense explained that it was the sports gloves, elbow, leg, and knee pads. Tossing them in the washer on the sanitize cycle with a bit of bleach will do the trick. Don't worry about ruining the sports pads. They will grow out of the gear before that happens.

---

[9] Momma out: That "I'm done" moment when you throw up your hands and take a walk.

High School

—◆◯◆—

Life moves pretty fast. If you don't stop
and look around once in a while,
you could miss it.
—Ferris Bueller, *Ferris Bueller's Day Off*

Decoding the Man-Cub

The documentary I mentioned earlier, *Raising Cain: Exploring the Inner Lives of America's Boys*, really helped me better understand the mental and physical development of the boys. It's a bit of a roller coaster as they zip from silly childish actions to a big man on campus.

One concept discussed in the second hour of the documentary was that if an immature male is confronted with something he did that negatively affects his perception of himself and his perceived idea of manhood, he will lie about it. The program also shared some case studies of how poor behavior and lying issues were identified and addressed.

The boys reacted differently to these types of instances. Earnest would clam up, and getting him to talk about the issue would be difficult. It might take several days for Earnest to put his thoughts together and share with Hon and me what he felt bad about. It was often that he forgot to turn in a homework assignment or hadn't effectively studied for a test. It took a lot of effort for us to come up with resolutions to an issue.

Exuberance, on the other hand, would bounce around, blaming the rest of the world for the problem. He rarely wanted to admit his role or action in an issue. Learning how to own your actions is a slow process, and only through consistent parental messaging and eventual maturity did it stick. In both cases, I had to wait until they were ready to discuss what was up and stay calm during the conversation.

"I didn't feel like it!" was one of my least favorite man-cub excuses. I began to understand that what they were actually saying was "I don't understand how to do it" or "I have no time management skills and couldn't get around to it." Hon and I spent a lot of time helping them learn how to find answers, resources, and shared tools to better manage their time. Our goal was always to teach them how to do it, not to do it for them.

Playpen Playpen

There was a large tribe of busy man-cubs in our neighborhood. They were constantly on the move, inventing new ways to prove their manhood and scare the MOB. We were on high alert during those years and somehow still missed a lot. The gift of cell phones was discovering the videos on their social media accounts as they spun their skateboard down a steep hill, flipped off diving boards, and leaped off the roof of a house into a pool. If I only had a dollar for every time I begged Exuberance to "Think first. Just think," I'd be a very rich woman.

One summer, a particularly energetic group of man-cubs decided to dig a pit as a clubhouse in the woods. They called it The Penthouse, but I called it The Playpen for all the obvious reasons. It was a pit after all. For months, you'd see this gang of boys on their bikes with shovels and pickaxes, heading off to dig and work on the Penthouse. They were on a mission!

They dug a pit so big, you could have parked two cars in it and not see their roofs. I estimate it was about 10 x 10 feet wide by 6 feet deep. One of the most endearing things about the man-cub is their single-minded determination when they have a vision in mind. The not-so-endearing thing is there's little cause-effect in their decision-making.

When they were done digging, the man-cub gang was so excited about their pit that they doubled down on the name, calling it Penthouse Penthouse. Creativity was not their strong suit. One day, I asked the ringleader, Ranger, "How is Pool Pool doing?" He stared at me blankly. I explained, "It's been raining for two days. I just figured it was a pool by now." He did not appreciate my humor.

Believe it or not, Penthouse Penthouse was a coveted hangout among the neighborhood man-cubs, something that should be protected. The MOB began suspecting something was up when the man-cubs began talking like they were in *West Side Story* and were practicing their Sharks and Jets dance moves. It was difficult to take it all seriously, but two groups of boys were actually sparring over the Penthouse. The man-cubs pounded their chests, insults were thrown, and phallic shapes were carved on trees next to Penthouse Penthouse by the opposing man-cubs. The MOB called, "Time out!"

One of the tips in the *Raising Cain* documentary was that immature males have a bigger problem lying in front of their friends than they do to their parents. I wanted to see this in action, so I invited the mothers and boys to our house to discuss the attack on Penthouse Penthouse and how to resolve it. I encouraged the boys to talk and the moms to listen. Ranger, the leader of Penthouse Penthouse, explained how hard he and his tribe had worked to dig the pit and laid out the issue. The man-cubs matured a little bit that day as they explained why they did what they did and apologized to each other. *Raising Cain* was right. They didn't want to tell lies in front of each other. There was a bit of cowboy up as they owned their actions. The stigma of being a liar was a bigger threat than admitting what they could have done better.

The whole conversation probably took fifteen minutes, but the air was cleared, and in typical boy fashion, they all ran out the door to play basketball in the driveway. I announced it was time for MOB happy hour, and the mothers got to breathe too.

These Shark and Jet moments are bound to happen during the man-cub stage. Friendships, both kids and adults, can explode and dissolve forever if the issue is not addressed head-on, and video proof from cell phones and security cameras only increases the righteousness of those involved. I highly recommend getting in front of these problems, putting all relevant parties in one room, and pushing the boys to discuss and resolve it together, not the parents.

> **Tip: The Retaliator**
>
> Hon had a punishment philosophy that didn't make sense to me initially. Since he grew up with three brothers and five sisters, I deferred to his guideline that *the retaliator should receive the harsher punishment*. As he explained to the boys, there will always be a situation where you feel wronged. It might be an elbow in the ribs on the basketball court, pushing or teasing from another kid, or a teacher or boss that you disagree with. If you retaliate, you will be penalized. Life is not fair. This philosophy dovetailed nicely with my attitude of "solve the conflict yourself, boys." If you make me the judge, no one will be happy. The boys learned to navigate these life skirmishes when they were young, and it has enabled them to not overreact and be more thoughtful adults.

Encouraging Independence

Building independence in your children is a project that begins when they are young. One of those building blocks for our boys started with the first haircut, about age three, where they directed the stylist and had to live with their haircut decision. Encouraging and teaching them to communicate to an adult how they want their hair to look, actively participating in the process, and owning the result was a building block in the foundation for independence.

As parents, we had to find opportunities for independence as our children grew. These little moments of accepting responsibility for a mistake, owning their actions, and learning from them were critical to launching kind, civil, and productive men.

Experts call firstborns natural leaders, but I think it has more to do with having more opportunities to build confidence and independence at an early age. Exuberance was happy to let Earnest be in charge. He was fearless but far from independent. Family jobs like feeding the dog or getting the mail when he was young helped him participate, gain a level of independence, and receive praise. Did they do these activities without being reminded? Not a chance! As they dropped and broke dishes going into the dishwasher and shrunk my clothes as they tossed them in the dryer, I remember thinking, "This independence thing doesn't come cheap!"

As the boys got older, independence came in the form of managing their homework, picking up their room, and doing their own laundry. Their middle school had a babysitting certification, and Earnest jumped on that. He began to make money taking care of younger boys in our neighborhood. In high school, getting a driver's license offered many new opportunities to build independence and take responsibility for their own actions.

Becoming the Baby Sitter

As I've mentioned earlier, the boys loved it whenever we lined up a male babysitter. When they came of age to babysit, I sought out younger MOB members who might need a sitter and shared with them our experience with boy babysitters. Earnest was a popular sitter for elementary school boys. He'd show up with a remote-controlled car or Pokémon cards and happily keep the boys busy playing. It was meaningful to his psyche too. It gave him a boost in confidence during years when confidence-building activities were tough to find for a quiet kid. He had a small group of friends, was an average student, and was not very competitive when it came to sports. But he was an A+ babysitter and made serious cash doing it.

Exuberance, on the other hand, preferred pet sitting to children. I thought that whatever the responsibility was, it was important to push the boys to be in charge of other living things. An added bonus, in my opinion, for babysitting kids was that they might recognize that offspring takes effort and postpone being a father until they grow up.

Exuberance's first babysitting opportunity came on July 3, the traditional night of a big party for adults in our neighborhood. Families with little kids lined up sitters well in advance. One year, Ginny, a younger MOB member, called, hoping to get a sitter. Earnest was booked, and with a bit of persuasion, I convinced Exuberance, who was around age fifteen, to babysit for two seven-year-old boys. Truth be told, it was the money that finally made him agree.

Exuberance went down the street to babysit the boys, and the adults went off to the neighborhood party. Later that night, Exuberance came blasting through the door, "I'm never doing that again!"

"How come? What happened?" Hon and I asked.

"Well, I thought I'd tire the boys out. After a bit of sword fighting and a Nerf battle, we played hide-and-seek. I was it. I searched the house and yard for over an hour, looking for them and yelling for them to come out. Finally, they crawled out of a creek in the side yard. They had been lying in the mud laughing at me for an hour, and I only made $10!"

Hon, Earnest, and I were all howling by the end of the story. It was obvious he was terrified that he had lost the boys he was supposed to be watching. He stomped off to bed and said he was only watching pets from now on.

The next day, after shoring up the critical third pillar with sleep, he said he had overreacted and he would be willing to watch those boys again.

"Really? What changed?" I inquired.

"Well, Ms. Ginny stopped by when I was playing basketball outside. She said the boys reported that I was their favorite sitter! And that she didn't have enough cash last night, so she gave me some more money."

I chuckled as he walked away, as I was sure Exuberance was thinking, "Note to self: Do not play hide-and-go-seek with young boys. Stick to plastic swords and Nerf battles."

The Balance of Fun and Respecting Other Property

We lived in a fun, active neighborhood full of traditions, like the last day of the summer water battle at the bus stop mentioned earlier. Around Halloween, ghosting occurred. The kids left treats and candy in a paper bag on the doorstep. The bags were often decorated with stickers and the word "Boo!" After depositing the bag of treats, they would ring the doorbell and run.

Our house was well-known as a great ghosting recipient because the boys and Razel could be counted on to run after you. Moms would text me on the down-low ahead of time to make sure we were home and the boys were around. The doorbell would ring, and Earnest, Exuberance, and Razel would sprint outside to catch the candy givers. It was really funny.

Now and then, I'd let the boys know when someone was coming. They would hide in the bushes, holding Razel, and waiting for the right opportunity to surprise the other kids. Moms did a little behind-the-scenes coordination to make sure attacks and surprises were kept in the spirit of fun, and the game was not played on families that were resistant to the mayhem.

Manhunt was another neighborhood game that the Boys of the Spit played all summer, and Earnest would join in too. Manhunt is basically hide and seek where a smaller group hides, and everyone else seeks. Like many things the boys were into, they would take this game to the next level. Clothing was selected with hiding in mind, and Halloween makeup was pulled out to make their face dark. One boy even wore a ghillie suit[10] and was so well camouflaged that he would disappear when lying on the leaves and dirt.

---

[10] Ghillie suit: One of the many beloved male military items you discover as a MOB member. It's a head-to-toe outfit resembling Chewbacca that allows for superior hiding on the ground during manhunt.

These games would jump around the neighborhood, and sometimes, neighbors didn't appreciate the kids tearing around, screeching, and laughing. The MOB tried to direct the kids into receptive areas and ran interference with people who were not fans. I would ask these people, "Would you prefer they were inside watching television and playing video games?"

I would have similar conversations with people who complained when a pack of boys was walking or riding their bikes from place to place. The assumption, especially with parents of younger kids, was that there would be trouble if there were too many boys hanging out together. I'll admit the MOB had our hands full with many course corrections, but that's how they learned to respect property and each other. There were times when the Boys of the Spit went too far, discussions were had, lessons were learned, and boundaries were clarified and identified.

A rare moment of stillness for the Boys of the Spit and their little brothers.

Suspended Disbelief

Suspended disbelief is a television production term. It describes an understanding between the program and the audience to accept a scene or plot and suspend their disbelief that something would never happen. We've all had the experience of watching a sitcom as it goes too far and crosses the line from funny to stupid and no longer believable. We would talk about what point "it lost me" happens when we watched television together as a family.

An illustration of suspended disbelief was the *Walking Dead* TV series. For me, there was nothing believable. I was not a fan of horror and truly hated the series. I spent several years retreating to another room while Hon and the boys watched religiously, hooting and hollering at the gore. I had concerns that it was desensitizing the boys to violence and would harm them.

Hon would roll his eyes and explain, "They know what's real and what's not. Good grief! It's zombies! They're boys. This is what we do."

I eventually gave up and joined them in the family room to watch. Family bonding in an all-male house is not always easy. We still make a game out of watching TV and encourage full commentary of effective storytelling, which is easier now that programs can be paused and rewound.

We also flip back and forth between news channels to see how they are spinning the information and trying to peel back the layers of onscreen commentary to find the actual news. I think having skepticism of the truth in media is healthy. There was a lot of propaganda and false information served up as facts, and I always encouraged the boys to validate what they could and follow their gut as to what was the real story.

This concept is even more important as we enter the age of Artificial Intelligence (AI). In the past, it would take a professional graphic artist hours of hard work to change a photograph by removing wrinkles or adding an element that was not originally in the photo. Today, with AI graphic tools, the artist's imagination becomes reality in minutes. We can no longer "believe it with our own eyes or ears." Recently, we have come up with a family safe phrase for the kids and my parents to prevent them from being scammed. It is horrifying to hear stories about deep fakes swindling savings from families. Media education and conversation are our only good defense against bad agents.

> ### Tip: The First Job
>
> A first job teaches *so* many important life lessons! There are the basics like showing up when you are scheduled and dressing appropriately for the job. Have a good attitude and be respectful to other people. And then there's the financial part of making and managing money and taxes. Building work ethic is a process that starts young and may take many years to set. Giddyup!

Off to Work You Go!

My father lined up my first *real* job in between high school and college. I worked in a small factory that made woven-wood window shades and learned how to use a glue gun, rout, and stain wooden headboards, and assemble window shades. The small factory had less than ten women, and several were close to my age with little kids. To me, the hourly wage was much more than I made babysitting, but I understood it had to be difficult to support a family on that salary. I worked in that factory for two summers to help pay for college and left each fall with increased motivation to do well in my studies.

My dad got my brother a job working as a bricklayer's apprentice and on a furniture moving crew. Both of us knew what hard work looked like, and as I got older, I appreciated the lesson my father taught us with those physically demanding jobs.

Hon had similar experiences growing up, and we wanted our boys to have the same appreciation for hard work. I promised, "Find yourself a job, or I will." Sister Sense told me that keeping the boys busy was crucial for keeping them out of trouble, and both boys worked part-time and odd jobs during high school. I had a very low tolerance for the man-cubs lying around the house during the summer.

Earnest became certified as a lifeguard and worked at a popular pool one summer. He didn't lifeguard the next year, expressing that with his ADHD, the responsibility stressed him out, and he was afraid he'd miss something. When he didn't find a job for himself the following year, I lined up some weeding and mulching jobs in the neighborhood. Exuberance's first job was as a busboy at a local restaurant. From there, he worked as a salesman at a bike shop and a barback at another restaurant after graduating from high school.

Hon and I learned that we needed to ask others (bosses, parents, family, etc.) their opinions to get a sense of our children's etiquette and social skills as teens. The boys were not always chatty or polite to us, but they had solid *social motor*[11] skills with others. Exuberance's first boss and owner of the restaurant, Tom, told us a story about how he had sent him outside to clean the gum off the sidewalk in front of the restaurant. An older man came by and told Exuberance he should not be doing that work and that the business was taking advantage of him. Exuberance explained that he was fine with the work and tried to continue. Tom came out to see what was going on and explained he had scraped the gum off the sidewalk himself; there was nothing his employees did that he hadn't done. Tom told us he was proud of Exuberance, and that he continued to be respectful and polite during the entire confrontation with the older man.

---

[11] Social motor: Infants start with gross motor skills, learning how to move their bodies. Then fine motor skills, like picking up small things with their fingers. Social motor is what I call the rest of it, which is how to interact as a human with the world. As parents, teaching social motor skills is where we have a significant impact.

> **Tip: Spinning the Conversation Wheel**
>
> My family has always joked that our dinner conversations were the wheel of misfortune. A conversation management tip is to ask the quietest person at the table an interesting question. The quiet ones typically have an entire conversation going on in their head and just need a push to say something out loud.
>
> Here are a few examples of interesting questions:
>
> - What are the three things you are most proud of?
> - Can you think of a single event in your history that continues to impact your life today?
>   - For example, the COVID-19 pandemic impacted everyone around the world. What changed positively and negatively in our society?
>   - My example is the Tylenol scare of 1982, when someone added poison to bottles in stores. I think of it whenever I wrestle safety packaging off a plastic bottle of over-the-counter medicine and believe it is the cause of everything shrink-wrapped to death today.

Exuberance's Great Adventure

Since both boys had driver's licenses and we were trying to balance four schedules, Hon and I finally broke down and decided to get a third vehicle. Earnest was a senior in high school, and Exuberance was a sophomore. Summer was approaching with all four of us working in different directions. We went to a used car dealership and found a car as close to a tank as we could find. It was a seventeen-year-old sedan, older than both boys. "Hey," I said to the boys. "It's new to you!" The car offered us new leverage over the kids when trying to get them to toe the line, as no one wanted the keys of independent transportation taken away.

Earnest headed off to college in the fall, and the car stayed at home. Earnest's college was a few hours away, and he wanted Exuberance to visit for his siblings' weekend since he was a bit homesick. Hon and I discussed letting Exuberance visit and eventually decided that he had been showing signs of maturity, which we wanted to encourage, and allowed him to drive himself to visit Earnest at college.

As part of the negotiation, Exuberance and I set up a new app that allowed me to see where he was with geolocation. The trip day arrived, and Hon and I reviewed the rules and our expectations. Exuberance headed off for siblings' day as soon as school was over. I was busy at work and not really thinking about it when I received a call on my cell phone.

"This is Officer Cubbybear of the Pennsylvania State Police," said a serious voice. My heart stopped. Officer Cubbybear? Was this real, or was someone pranking me?

"Uh-huh," was all I could say.

"I just pulled over your son for speeding. Is he old enough to drive? He says he is but can't find his license. He was doing ninety-eight miles an hour on the Pennsylvania Turnpike."

"What? How fast was he going? He does have a driver's license."

"Ninety-eight miles an hour, ma'am."

"Scare him!" I shouted into the phone. "Scare him." There was silence on the other end of the phone. Apparently, "Scare him," was not a typical parental response.

"Ma'am, he says his license might be in his bedroom. If you can find it and can share a photo, I'll use it when I write up the ticket."

"Officer, have you seen a teenage male's bedroom lately? I think it's unlikely, but my husband is home, and I'll see if he can find it. My husband will call Exuberance back in a few minutes. Thank you for pulling him over."

I started stalker-calling Hon, who did not pick up. First, the house phone and, next, his cell until he finally answered a phone. He had gotten off work early and was taking a nap. I explained that Officer Cubbybear was with our stupid and reckless boy. Hon went off to look for the driver's license and promised to call me back after speaking to the officer.

He called me after hanging up the phone with Exuberance and Officer Cubbybear. Hon could not locate the license, but somehow, the officer was able to confirm that our son's Maryland license did exist. Hon thanked the officer and reassured him that we were not taking the issue lightly. The officer expressed that it was refreshing to talk with parents who were not trying to make excuses for their children. He issued Exuberance a ticket. Hon thanked the officer and asked him to have Exuberance call him before he went anywhere.

Hon said to Exuberance, "Here's what you're going to do. I want you to drive to the next exit and get off. Then make a left over the highway and get back on the highway going the opposite direction."

"You mean I'm not going to be able to go to siblings' weekend? I'm almost there," whined Exuberance.

"No," said Hon. "That opportunity is not happening. And I know how far away you are and know how to calculate how long it will take you to travel at the speed limit. Do not go one mile over the limit, do you understand?"

Hon called Earnest next to explain that Exuberance would no longer be coming to visit. Earnest shared that he had been listening over Exuberance's speakerphone to the entire police stop, then commented, "Dad, I don't know how he got the car up to that speed! It always starts shaking when I get it over eighty miles per hour."

"Eighty! What are you doing? That car is seventeen years old. You can't drive it that fast!" exclaimed Hon.

For the next few hours, I watched Exuberance slowly return home on the geolocation app. Since it was late and we were all devoid of patience, we decided to talk about it the next day. The next morning, I got Exuberance up and told him he needed to clean his room, then the car, and find his license. It turned out it was stuck in the car driver's seat, and he had been sitting on it the entire time.

There was much discussion about how to discipline him, and several people encouraged us to get a lawyer and fight the ticket. We did not get a lawyer, and we made Exuberance call the courthouse to figure out how to take care of the ticket himself. As I recall, the speeding fine was a few hundred dollars, which he paid for himself. It took many hours of bussing tables to pay for that fine, and he was limited to bicycle transportation for a while.

Exuberance was the kind of teenage boy that had to learn lessons the hard way. He had so much excitement, energy, and testosterone that thinking first did not come easily. We were all lucky that his speeding adventure didn't end tragically, and we will be forever grateful to that officer who pulled him over. Exuberance learned so many lessons from that "adventure" that he shared it in his college applications essay.

> ### Tip: The Rules of Adventure
>
> After Exuberance's great adventure, Hon came up with travel rules. He based his list on just three things knowing that was all the boys would remember. These were our expectations when the boys went on adventures, overnights, and vacations with other families.
>
> 1. We do not want to hear from healthcare professionals.
> 2. We do not want to hear from law enforcement professionals.
> 3. We expect you to leave destinations and return things (cars, people, etc.) that you took with you in better shape than when you left. Until they were independent, they understood things included them.

Technology: The Struggle Is Real

I encourage you to monitor computers, phones, house cameras, social media, etc., and embrace the tools that will help you keep your children safe. We installed a security camera at the front of the house when the boys were in middle school to keep track of their comings and goings. By high school, I found it entertaining that if we were out, their friends would sneak in through the basement door to avoid the cameras but would forget when they left and walk out the front door. As a submarine parent, I typically was on to their shenanigans and would confront them about what was afoot.

With the state of media today, I think it's important to teach our kids media literacy basics and understand that it's all a very profitable business. Television, podcasts, and streaming programs are created to elicit emotions. They get viewers and revenue through commercials and sponsors. Boring programming doesn't make money. The goal of media organizations is to attract loyal viewers. If a program is getting you or your kids spun up, it's time to pause, ask why, and do a bit of fact-checking.

Teaching and understanding the impact of privacy and notification settings on your electronic devices is another challenge for parents and teens. It's hard to ignore the ding of your phone and the message tease to get your attention. I recommend turning off as many notifications on their devices as possible and utilizing tools like *favorites* to prioritize what can get through.

Clickbait is another example of this type of communication where a headline is designed to be outrageous to get you to open the link. I tried to show my boys how to manage their device notifications and privacy settings, so they could be in better control of the clickbait that might interrupt their attention.

As I explained to the boys, there is nothing in the parenting handbook that says we need to supply internet access 24/7 or provide a television in your room. It just isn't in the parent-child contract. All the technology in our house was closely monitored. I actively used the program that came with our cable provider to manage the Wi-Fi and devices on our network. It allowed me to identify every device, assign them to a user, and curtail access. During high school, this enabled me to set up a schedule where Exuberance's Wi-Fi access ended earlier than Earnest's. I could also adjust the schedule as grades and behavior ebbed and flowed. Wi-Fi access was on a schedule that, on school nights, it was turned off at 11:00 p.m. and was on at 6:00 a.m. with few exceptions.

As a highly mediocre parent, I did not feel the need to be tech support and pushed the boys to figure out solutions for themselves. Earnest loved reading and was given one of the first-generation Kindles when he was a man-cub. Unfortunately, he was not great at taking care of his technology, and within a month of receiving it, he fell asleep reading one night and rolled over on it, breaking the screen. He was devastated. I set him up on the speakerphone in the kitchen while I made dinner and had him call Amazon support.

"Earnest, play the kid card. Amazon sees you as a possible lifelong customer and will want to make you happier than if I called them," I explained. "Besides, it's your Kindle. You broke it. Now fix it."

Success! He convinced Amazon to send him a new Kindle more than once because, as a man-cub, it takes a bit for you to understand you need to move your device to the bedside table before you fall asleep. Earnest was so good at talking to tech support that he had a similar conversation at the Apple Genius Bar after he dropped his new iPad and shattered the screen. Apple too understood who their future customer base was and replaced it at no expense. These experiences taught Earnest to be responsible for his personal assets, to take better care of them, and to advocate for himself with large companies.

Identifying Earnest's natural ability to discuss technology on the phone, I saw an opportunity to share my tech support obligations with my parents and put him on the phone with Nana to help her with her iPad. She was much more responsive to him than she was to me. I could whisper suggestions to him that he would pass along. He was so good at tech support that older residents in our neighborhood would hire him by the hour to teach them how to use their mobile devices and computers. Win-win!

Extracurricular Activities

I am a professional spectator. My brother broke me in with lacrosse and football, but the boys seemed to try them all—karate, baseball, basketball, scouts, sailing, camp, soccer, lacrosse, chess club, fencing, swimming, cross country, and robotics. A busy boy is the key to MOB sanity, and joining a carpool is the way you get it done.

Fencing was probably the shortest-lived extracurricular activity. Even though on the surface it seems like the perfect activity for Exuberance, combining a weapon and a sport, the fact was that he needed to master the lunge before being handed a sword. After several classes of sore legs from lunging and still no weapon, he called Uncle and moved on to the next sport.

Earnest discovered his love for robotics in middle school with Lego Mindstorm and was excited to learn that the high school had a robotics program. It was the only extracurricular activity that Earnest participated in during all four years. The high school program built a variety of robots and competed with other schools. When Earnest joined the club as a freshman, the program was in its infancy and did not have much adult support. He had fun, but the team had limited success. By his junior year, Hon and I could no longer stand by and watch the kid's disappointment as the team failed to complete their builds in time to compete. We both stepped in and volunteered to help the faculty supervisors and the club. I taught and provided them with project management support: how to identify the stages of development and create a schedule that allowed for the robots to be built, tested, and develop improvements by competition time. The club was also underfunded by the school and did not have the financial commitment of school sports and a booster club. Hon identified a STEM grant, and the club members wrote a grant request proposal and were awarded over $1,000 for equipment and supplies.

During robotics competitions, students were required to wear long-sleeved shirts with collars and a tie. The club really didn't feel like a team, so I convinced the club administrator to let me help them brand the club. The students designed a logo, and we ordered long-sleeve-collared shirts in the school colors with the logo for each club member. The pride on their faces as they tried on their new shirts was heartwarming. They excitedly proclaimed that they could wear their uniforms just like the athletic kids on competition days. The shirts, the STEM grant, and the newfound project management leadership skills seemed to increase their pride in the school and themselves.

Hon and my goal were not to take over the club but rather to work with the school and administrators when we volunteered. The effort that Earnest and his team put into creating a solid foundation for the future of the club, which continued to win STEM grants, and is very successful today.

Earnest's high school robotics club members proudly wear their new team shirts.

Exuberance loved sports and envisioned himself as an all-American lacrosse player, but since he didn't have a growth spurt until junior year, he did not make the JV team. Instead, he shifted his attention to cross country and ran on the team all four years of high school. I knew nothing of the sport when he started, and now I have great respect for it. Unlike other sports, which can be cliquey and political, cross country is all about the best time. If you run fast enough, you're on the team; faster still, and you're in the first heat.

It's an individual sport and the team is coed, so everybody cheers for each other and celebrates teammates success. It had a different vibe than all-male sports.

The heats were about twenty minutes long, and spectators would hustle from point to point to catch a glimpse of their child from the starting line, deep in the woods, and finish line. It was active for runners and spectators alike.

The most important thing for both boys was to find their tribe. It was different for each child, and I did not try to force friend overlap. There were very few people that both boys were friends with. Earnest made lifelong friends in robotics and learned critical project management and computer design skills, which he still uses today in his profession. Exuberance, with his boundless energy, became a supportive team member and solid competitor on the school's cross-country team.

Navigating Adolescent Anguish and Emotional Health

There's no sugarcoating it. The adolescent stage is a bit terrifying. Parenting decisions do not always come easy, and we really need to rely on the trust we built with our sons over a lifetime to make the right moves.

Another thing about this period is the emotional spillover from other children struggling to find their way. Both boys experienced and were worried about friends who were depressed and harming themselves during their middle and high school years. One of the boys' friends tried to commit suicide, and another friend died. Both events and others rippled grief and shock throughout our community. As a parent, you will likely have to deal with these realities too and decide what is the best course of action to support your child and the community. Hon and I both encouraged the boys to talk with us and, when we couldn't connect, asked aunts, uncles, and professionals to help.

There were two different times I had to call a parent and share with them that their child was cutting themselves. The boys were concerned that I would damage the trust of their friend. I explained that there were some problems that were above the kid's pay grade and that this was a complicated situation even for an adult. I asked them to trust me to do the right thing and let them know I was going to call the parents and share what I knew. Also, I tried to explain that their friend was asking for help with an act like cutting. We, both adults and friends, would not ignore their pain and would help and support them.

I recognize that calling another parent and voicing your concerns about their child can be a volatile situation. I tried to convey that we had only the best of intentions and strove to reach out with compassion and concern. During those difficult conversations, the parents were grateful and appreciated that we were comrades in parenting, and I was not judging.

I tried to explain to the boys that their friends were depressed and in an emotional pit. "You can't climb into the pit to help them. The only thing you can do is offer a hand to help them out. You can't change them, but you can offer your support and compassion."

We also made sure the boys had a mental health professional to discuss these complicated issues of maturity. We called it *mental floss*, and every now and then, we all need a bit of flossing. Throughout their lives, we relied on professionals to help us when we were overwhelmed as parents. I typically called these professionals *coaches*, a term they understood from a young age. Child psychiatrists were called life coaches, and we didn't get much pushback from either boy when we lined up appointments. As they matured, they often asked me to make an appointment for them.

I do not understand why our health and insurance system seems to have such an issue with paying mental health professionals, but we never managed to find someone in our insurance plan who was a good fit and always had to pay out of pocket. That money was an investment I'd make any day of the week. It was more important to us to find someone who clicked with the boys than a professional in our insurance plan. During the middle and high school time frame, we had Adam the Boy Whisperer on speed dial. Ms. Gail was our mental health lifeline when they were younger and helped navigate Earnest's ADHD.

I also confided in the school guidance counselors when things got sticky to make sure someone at school was aware of what was going on. Guidance counselors are unsung heroes in public schools, and we were blessed to have amazing counselors for both boys. In high school, we had an incredibly talented and kind woman as the boy's guidance counselor. She helped navigate 504 plans, the repercussions of a friend trying to commit suicide, slipping grades, and college applications. She invited me into her office when I was in a panic, not knowing how to traverse the most recent batch of MOB life. She offered advice, talked with the boys, explained the tools that were available in the school, and sat in on meetings with teachers and administrators. I will forever be grateful.

Have Faith! Your Village Is Larger than You Think

During these difficult times, we also confided in our families and close friends. We recognized the importance of helping the boys focus on the future and build independence. A particularly trying summer following Earnest's senior year in high school, Hon's younger brother, Mike, arranged an internship with the company where he worked. It was a software development shop that was developing facial recognition software for security solutions. Earnest would spend a few nights a week with Mike's family and work with him during the day. One of the jobs Earnest did was as a test subject. He would walk in zigzag patterns while contorting his face to see if the facial recognition software could identify him. I used to tease him that he needed to watch out in the airport, or he might be identified as test subject 4.

The internship that summer was transformative for Earnest. Mike and his wife had two younger children. Earnest got to know his cousins better and would babysit here and there too. The family lived in Virginia, on the other side of DC from us. Because traffic is legendarily horrible, we would drop Earnest off at a subway on our side of DC, and they would pick him up in their town. Earnest learned how to pack his essentials for a few days, travel on public transportation, and live with another family. These were impactful building blocks for independence and getting ready for his next chapter, going away to college.

There were other champions for the boys. Seemingly, one of Earnest's best friends during middle and high school was his bus driver, Mr. C. He welcomed the quiet kids to the front of the bus where they discussed interesting topics and solved the world's problems. During the holidays, I would buy gift cards at the local coffee shop and let each boy give them to the people who helped them the most. It was up to them to choose to whom they showed gratitude.

Recognizing that Hon and I were not experts in all things, we also had a slew of tutors to fill in when we weren't a good fit for the problem at hand. Earnest struggled with executive functioning and organization, and we found him an organizational coach. Mr. Mac came once a week for a few years during high school to help him plan his assignments, sort through his backpack, and learn critical scheduling skills. As an added bonus, Mr. Mac was also an English teacher and helped Earnest become a very strong writer.

Exuberance made use of a math and science tutor in our neighborhood, Ms. Robin. She jumped in when he didn't understand a lesson and even tutored him via video conference while he was off in college.

Even though I have a can-do attitude, I have always understood my limitations. And there are times, like teaching the boys to play guitar, when even though I was capable of it, they were not going to learn from me as well as from another musician. The key was to have faith that there were other talented and giving souls if you took the time to find them.

Graduation Is Around the Bend

Around their senior year of high school, my man-cubs started pulling away. I was suddenly the shortest person in the family and working hard to retain control from my lower vantage point. As with most of these boy milestones, Earnest transitioned from stage to stage slowly and quietly. Exuberance, in contrast, was constantly pushing boundaries and in a hurry to catch up to Earnest.

Spring break, junior year of high school, seemed to be the point when we visited colleges. We utilized the college prep information from the public school's guidance portal to try to come up with a short list of colleges to visit. Choosing what you want to do after high school is one of the first adult decisions a young person gets to make. I thought it was important to help teach them how to make a big decision, and I updated a decision matrix tool of my father's to help the boys understand what they were looking for in higher education.

The first step was to have them identify up to eight features that they were looking for in a college, personal priorities, and rank them from the most important (8) to the least important (1).

PERSONAL PRIORITIES	RANK (8 best 1 least)
Vibe	7
Tuition	6
Majors & Courses	8
Dorms	3
Size of the School	2
Distance from Home	5
Clubs and Extracurriculars	4
Town	1

After we visited each school, I'd ask them to evaluate it based on their personal priority from 4 (best) to 1 (worst) and add that 1 to 4 score to the yellow box. Then I multiplied the priority ranking and the school's score to get a subtotal which was written in the blue box. The blue box subtotals were then added up to create a total score for the school. The total is a weighted score based on their priorities and rankings. As we visited schools, the ones that seemed like good matches for the boys revealed themselves in the matrix.

PERSONAL PRIORITIES

Yellow Box: Rank each school against the priority on a scale of 1 (worst) to 4 (best). Blue Box: Multiply the green priority with the yellow ranking and write in blue box.	Majors & Courses	Vibe	Tuition	Distance from Home	Extracurriculars	Dorms	Size of School	Town	Add up weighted scores in blue box and write total in this column.
ALTERNATIVES	8	7	6	5	4	3	2	1	**TOTALS**
School #1	3	3	2	4	2	3	3	2	102
	24	21	12	20	8	9	6	2	
School #2	4	2	3	3	4	3	4	3	115
	32	14	18	15	16	9	8	3	
School #3									

We also created a second spreadsheet with the cost per year of each school. Hon and I believed the boys should have skin in the game and fully understand the cost of higher education. We agreed to pay for three years, and they needed to pay for one year. The costs per year part of the spreadsheet is more complicated than you'd imagine because each school seemed to have a different way of breaking down the expenses. Understanding the total cost of attending a college helped us all make an informed decision. Exuberance changed from an expensive out-of-state private university to an in-state school after understanding that both schools had similar total scores, but the cost per year was significantly different. He recognized that he didn't want a school loan that was double the cost of the state school. It was a huge relief to Hon and me that he reached this reality on his own, as we couldn't afford to pay for the other three years either.

COST PER YEAR

SCHOOL	TUITION	ROOM & BOARD	OTHER FEES (BOOKS, ETC.)	FINANCIAL AID/ MERIT MONEY	TOTAL COST
School #1	$11,084	$13,900	$1,300	-$5,000	$21,284
School #2	$22,174	$14,300	$1,300	-$0	$37,774
School #3	$48,700	$19,606	$1,300	-$23,000	$46,606

Exuberance went along to nearly all of Earnest's college visits, which helped motivate him to stay focused in high school and exposed both of them to a possible higher education future. Earnest was focused on a school with some type of engineering. After visiting one of the college open houses, Exuberance explained that he was excited that he could go to college undeclared. He had been worried about not knowing what he was interested in, and we had a lively car conversation about the difficulty of selecting a career right out of high school.

Teaching the boys how to make an important decision, like selecting a college, was a critical milestone in their independence and self-confidence. Hon and I tried to make it fun and not confrontational. We shared our experiences and explained how it's important to get the training they need, whether it's higher education or trade school, to set themselves up for financial independence and success. (Visit the mothersofboys.life website for the decision matrix.)

As I think back to when I went to college, I am astounded at the difference in the cost of higher education today. I went to a state school as an out-of-state student for under $4,000 a year in the 1980s. That same school costs over $27,000 a year today for an out-of-state student. Hon and I calculate that we have invested over $180,000 in our boys' education, and they are paying another $25,000 each. This was only accomplished through hard work and loans. My parents' generation didn't have to choose between investing in their retirement savings and their children's education. Hon and I were both able to contribute to our college education by working during the summer, and any small loans were paid off shortly after graduation. Today, the cost of higher education is significant, and I encourage you and your family to discuss all options openly and honestly.

AP Classes and Community College

Earnest needed only one class for graduation in his senior year, English. To fill up his schedule, he signed up for three Advanced Placement (AP) classes and began the school year full of confidence. By November, the course load required for the AP classes was crushing him. He was depressed and overwhelmed from trying to keep up. We worked to get him tutors and scheduled a meeting with the school since he had a 504 plan to help with his ADHD. Nothing seemed to help. I asked if we could drop two of the AP classes since they were not required for graduation, which was going to kill his GPA, and might negatively affect his applications for colleges. The high school said that it didn't work like college and that dropping the classes was not allowed until the third semester. I was not happy with that answer.

Continuing to advocate for my man-cub, I scheduled a meeting with the principal and made sure Hon was going to come with me. We sat in the principal's office and discussed Earnest's situation of overcommitting himself with the AP classes, causing all his grades to drop and making him feel hopeless and overwhelmed. The principal understood our concerns but insisted that it was a board of education policy and was out of his hands. I calmly explained that we were not leaving until we had identified a solution, and waiting until the third semester to drop two classes wasn't it. We sat for a very long moment in silence. The principal looked at Hon for help, and he shrugged as if to say, "Did you notice she has red hair? We're not going anywhere until there's a solution." The principal finally said he would allow Earnest to drop two of the three AP classes and set him up to intern in the office and the tech ed with his spare school time. Hon and I thanked him and left.

I found that logic and calm determination were a combination that worked with the schools and educators. We respected and supported teachers and the schools, and I expected them to do the same. The reduced course load ensured that Earnest was successful in his senior year and gave him more tools for his next chapter.

We also realized a couple of things about AP classes that we didn't repeat with Exuberance. The college-level classes are taught by high school teachers. At the end of the year, students can pay for and take a national test to potentially receive college credit. The national test does not take into account any issues the teacher may have had in completing the material or other limitations, like lost teaching days due to snow; it is the same highly challenging test across the country. Students' tests are graded on a scale from one to five, and they *may* earn college credit if they receive a three or higher. Not all colleges accept AP credits, and it is entirely up to their discretion. Earnest's college did not accept many of his AP credits.

Exuberance never took more than one AP class at a time. Instead, we focused on honors classes where he could be more successful and confident. In his senior year, we registered him for a program called Jump Start, which allowed him to take classes at our local community college in addition to the few courses needed for graduation. It was one of our most successful decisions. Since he was hanging out with older kids, he needed to behave like a college kid to fit in. This experience allowed him to avoid much of "senioritis," get a taste of college-level material, and gain the confidence he needed to make decisions about his future. In contrast to our AP class experiences, all his community college credits transferred, and he started college with twelve credits.

Firecracker and Rockets

Earnest and Exuberance had incredibly different personalities as their nicknames illustrate. It didn't mean that I was less worried about the actions of one over the other. Earnest often floated under the radar, but he was still drawn to dangerous things that Hon and I worked to support responsibly and not dismiss.

Earnest's birthday was in late June, and every year, he saved his gift money to buy fireworks, then begged us to take him to a state that sold a better selection. He was persistent and patient with his determination to shoot off rockets. Hon and I had our jobs cut out for us as we tried to find safe places to light off fireworks and launch rockets.

The other challenge was keeping teenage Exuberance and the Boys of the Spit from stealing Earnest's fireworks. The Boys of the Spit did not have patience, and the MOB parents occasionally had to crack down on the unsanctioned use of fireworks when Earnest was in college, leaving his stash unprotected.

During the man-cub phase, the boys seemed continuously drawn to danger. Their risk analysis abilities were marginalized by the testosterone flowing through their bodies. Don't presume that the quiet one is less likely to be in trouble. We leaned heavily on our community to inform us when things got out of hand. Without the casual "Hey, I don't know if you are aware, I think I saw your son riding on the roof of a car through the hood" in the grocery store from a neighbor, we may have been in the dark. "See something, say something" applies to man-cubs too.

Leaping Forward

This parenting thing is not for the light of the heart. It's inevitable that your child will do things that terrify you. The Boys of the Spit called themselves the idiots, and no one in the MOB disagreed. Exuberance was an early adopter of leaping and was happy to jump into a risky idea. Today, he thinks it's funny to identify the bridges in our area that the idiots jumped off. I've had to ask him to stop sharing.

During high school, I actively followed him and his friends on social media in true submarine parenting style to get a clue as to what they were up to. As the tech mom, I shared the intel with the rest of the MOB. Below are still frames of a video I discovered on Instagram. Exuberance was on vacation with a girlfriend and her family.

I don't really have any advice except to say that the immature male brain is not good at identifying risk. I'd like to think that our conversations after being pulled over by Officer Cubbybear and addressing general stupid behavior made a difference, but the truth is that I don't think Exuberance realized potential consequences until afterward. Thankfully, they do mature. The only thing we could do as parents is make him understand that for every action, there is an equal and opposite reaction. There would be consequences. I continued to beg, "*Think*. Just think," as he headed out the door.

Talking with Your Man-Cub about Alcohol

Hon and I had several discussions on how to prepare Earnest to leave the nest and go to college. In Maryland, there is a crazy tradition where graduates head off for a week at the beach immediately following high school graduation. These adventures are typically without adult supervision. Senior Week was something I remember fondly after graduation. Hon was concerned that if we let Earnest go, we'd need to let Exuberance participate, and that was a whole different kettle of fish.

I wasn't sure Earnest would even want to go, but when he came to us and asked us if he could go to the South Carolina shore with a group of friends and a dad, we immediately said, "Yes!" Earnest recently confided that our encouragement of him to go on that trip was a big step in his mental confidence to leave for college later that summer.

Earnest was not a partier, which was great, but it made Hon and I concerned that he did not understand alcohol and its effects. Hon and I found an evening when Exuberance was not around to discuss it with Earnest. "You are heading off to college in a few weeks," Hon began. "That was a pretty exciting time for me. When I was a freshman, I was legal to drink in the state of New Jersey."

I chimed in, "The drinking age in Maryland was eighteen for beer and wine. But I went to school in Pennsylvania where it was twenty-one. A few years later, the law was changed to twenty-one in nearly every state. Have you tasted much alcohol?"

Earnest shook his head and said, "Only a bit of beer."

"Since Exuberance isn't around tonight, we want to talk about the different proofs of alcohol," explained Hon. "Chances are that you are going to be exposed to alcohol in college. The biggest thing to understand is that the amount of alcohol is rated on a scale called proof. They get the proof by multiplying the volume of alcohol by two."

Hon continued, "You need to understand how strong the beverage is to appreciate the effect on your body. Beer is on the low end of the proof scale with about 5 percent alcohol or 10 proof. Wine is more than twice the proof of beer, about 12 percent alcohol or 24 proof. Vodka, whiskey, rum, tequila, and other spirits start at 40 percent alcohol or 80 proof. As you might imagine, the higher the proof, the stronger the effect. How many beers would you need to drink to equal a glass of wine?"

Earnest smiled, thrilled to be having such an adult discussion. "You'd need to drink two beers to keep up with one glass of wine."

I chime in, "Many adults don't understand how this works. I had this discussion recently with a friend who was ordering a glass of wine with each Guinness beer I ordered. Guinness is low in alcohol, about 4 percent, and low-calorie beer. You'd have to drink three Guinness to have the same amount of alcohol in a glass of wine. I order it when I want to be social but do not want to feel the effects of alcohol. My friend didn't believe me at first, thinking that because it was dark, it was high in alcohol. I explained that the color only meant the grains were roasted longer. She was shocked when Dr. Google confirmed my statement. There's also a type of beer called malt liquor. I got myself in trouble once when I was young because I didn't realize it was a higher 14 proof compared with beer that's about ten proof. I didn't understand that a few numbers could have such a significant effect. It did."

Hon poured two small glasses, one with whiskey and the other with vodka. "I want you to smell and take a small taste of these," he said, handing the glasses to Earnest. "What do you smell? What do you taste? With your picky taste buds, you could easily be a connoisseur when you're older."

Earnest smelled each and took little sips. "The vodka has no smell at all and very little taste. The whiskey, on the other hand, has an earthy, woody smell and much stronger taste."

Hon said, "That's right. They are both eighty proof, but you might not realize how much vodka you drank if you weren't paying attention because there's not much taste to it."

I jumped in. "You are going to go to school in Pennsylvania like I did. When I was in college, they used to have parties with a punch that had grain alcohol in it. Grain is 190 proof, more than twice as strong as vodka or other spirits. What do you think happened to kids that didn't understand how strong grain is?"

Earnest replied with a concerned look, "They would get really drunk."

"That's right," I said. "Which can be very dangerous. I knew someone in college who died because they drank too much. When I went off to college, I weighed about a hundred pounds. Let's say you and I were at a party as freshmen, and we were drinking the same amount of beer. Three beers in, what difference do you think there would be?"

"Well, I'm a lot bigger and heavier than you. I guess you'd be twice as drunk as me," said Earnest.

"I'm not sure it would be twice as much, but body weight plays a big part in how alcohol affects you. Also, how many drinks you might have over a period of time. You will meet girls and boys when you are at college who might not understand the effects of alcohol. There are also boys and men who will take advantage of a drunk woman. I know you are not that kind of man, and I want you to do a favor for me. If you see someone who has had too much to drink and is not able to take care of themselves, do the honorable thing like Cowboy Ben talked about when you were young. Help them get back to their dorm and turn them over to someone who can keep an eye on them."

Earnest nodded, absorbing all this conversation.

"Oh," I concluded, "your brother, Exuberance, falls into this category because he is a knucklehead. Take care of him too."

Earnest and Hon chuckled and nodded at that comment because I was right.

Hon and I didn't appreciate how important this conversation was at that moment. Looking back, it helped the three of us move to more equal footing. Earnest felt as though he was being treated as an adult, and we were having an adult conversation, which we were.

We had a similar conversation with Exuberance before he flew the nest to college. He, as the second born, thought he already knew it all. Hon and I expressed our expectations of his behavior, knowing that he was going to push the boundaries much further.

Earnest called me a few weeks into his freshman year of college, excited to report, "Mom, I took care of a drunk girl last night and made sure she got back to her dorm."

"I knew you would. Earnest, I'm proud of you for being one of the men I greatly respect." He couldn't see me, but I was beaming from ear to ear, knowing I helped raise a capable, compassionate man.

The Remarkable Transformation

Love many, trust few, always paddle your own canoe.
—Grammie

> **Tip: Turning Eighteen, a Legal Adult**
>
> Just in Case: When your man-cub turns eighteen, he will legally be an adult and able to vote, enlist in the military, and make his own medical decisions. Before the boys went off to college, we had them sign a Power of Attorney (POA) and an advanced medical directive (a.k.a. health care proxy), giving us the right to talk to medical professionals and act on their behalf if they are unable to communicate for themselves or need our assistance.

Earnest Leaves the Nest

During this time, I realized Hon and I had been slowly changing our language with Earnest. "You must" became "I suggest" or "I recommend." We tried to limit detailed instructions and, instead, encouraged him to figure it out. And on occasion, offered, "You might want to consider" as a recommendation. When we had questions, we began the conversation with "Help me understand" to give him the benefit of the doubt that he had made a good decision. Good decision-making is a slowly evolving skill where successes and failures are recognized.

Moving Earnest into college was a full family affair. We all piled into the car for the drive to his university. According to Sister Sense, packing and preparing for college was much easier for boys than if we had a girl. With the boys, there was no preplanned coordination between roommates regarding who was bringing what or a color scheme. The hardest thing about getting ready was finding the extra-long twin sheets. Earnest had limited suggestions for what he wanted to bring, so I picked up what I thought was important.

I did go into a big box store and purchased an empty first aid kit container and filled it with the old standbys: Band-Aids, antibiotic ointment, Ace bandage, and new additions: fingernail clippers, tweezers, Benadryl, and ibuprofen. Earnest later reported back that he was known in his dorm for having a first aid kit and met several friends who came to his door in need.

It was an emotional day for all of us. Even Exuberance was on the emotional pendulum of "I finally get to be an only child!" to "Oh no! *All* of my parents' attention will turn to me because I will be the only child at home!"

Earnest and Exuberance in the backseat on the way to Earnest's first year at college.

One of my jobs during college was student staff for freshman orientation. I remember talking with parents and advising them to try to encourage their children to stay at school and not come home until Thanksgiving break. Homesickness is a common occurrence until they become comfortable with their new environment. Coming home on the weekends would only prolong the homesick time period.

Following Christmas break in January, they would be begging to go back to school and ready to return to their new normal.

Earnest was a shy guy, slow to make friends, and homesick. I had to listen to my nineteen-year-old son and help him become settled. We had regular calls and encouraged him to stay put and join in the freshman social activities. We sent care packages and suggested the grandparents reach out to him too. Exuberance, Hon, and I piled in the car and went to visit him for his parents' weekend, and another time, Hon went by himself for some one-on-one time. Earnest and Hon still talk about what a great visit that was. By Thanksgiving, Earnest was in a new groove and comfortable with his college life. And by the end of Christmas break, he was excited to go back to his life at college.

Sister Sense—Care Package Party

A care package party is a fun activity to fill the hole left in your life when your man-cub leaves the nest. Bonding with other families with children the same age was good for the soul. I included the dads too, who also enjoyed it, and always made a big pot of chili or soup for a potluck dinner.

Here is how it works for six care packages/families:

- Stop by the post office and pick up six medium Priority Mail boxes (free).
- Instruct all families to bring six of a particular item. For example, six boxes of Band-Aids or six decks of cards. Get creative.
- Pass around the boxes so that each family adds their item to the box.
- Ship! The kids always loved the variety, and we often included a group message of encouragement and support.

Loss of Razel

Razel, our beloved dog and the only other girl in the house, sadly got old. She was such a staple of our family and an excellent communicator. There was never a doubt about what she wanted. She helped teach the boys responsibility and let them know when her dinner or water bowl was empty, and when it was time to go outside. As she aged and moving was tougher, at night, she would push her bed and whine until we moved it into her desired sleeping spot where she could watch both the front door and the hallway to the bedrooms. She was still on guard.

Razel thoughtfully waited for Earnest to return home from college before she decided it was time to cross the rainbow bridge. Although she thought the time was right, I was not ready for it. She chose the day of my colonoscopy, and I was lying on the couch with a screaming headache as I waited for my appointment time.

"Mom, Razel is not eating, drinking, or going out," said Exuberance. "She's panting. Today is my first day of work at the bike shop, and I have to leave soon. What should we do?"

I peeled myself off the couch to check on Razel. Exuberance and I slipped a towel under her and tried to get her on her feet together. She was not interested in getting up, and her look at me said she was done. Earnest walked in. He had been recruited to drive me to my colonoscopy appointment, and it was time to leave. We all gave Razel some love, and Earnest told her he'd be right back.

I called the vet on the way to the doctor's appointment and tried unsuccessfully to convince them to stay open until Exuberance and Hon got home from work. They gave me the number of a vet service that comes to the house, and I begged the woman on the phone from the gurney as they were about to take me away for the procedure to please find us a vet that could come after 7:00 p.m. It was a sh—t show from so many angles.

While I was getting my colonoscopy, a vet was magically found and agreed to come to our house that night at 7:30 p.m. When

Earnest and I returned home, Razel was relieved to hear we had worked everything out.

Her passing was really quite beautiful. The vet came to the house and had a special blanket that was put under Razel. We were all around her bed as she drifted off to sleep. She was at peace. Hon and the boys each took a corner of the blanket and carried her to the vet's car. Her ashes returned in a beautifully carved rosewood box. It was the dignified end that Razel coordinated and deserved, and she helped teach the boys about the circle of life. We still miss her so.

The Value of Research and Advice

When I was in my twenties, I owned an old row house in Baltimore that needed a lot of work. Since YouTube hadn't been invented, there were only two ways to learn how to renovate: books and Subject Matter Experts (SMEs). I learned the value of research and asking experts during those years.

One day, I decided to make a long brick planter in my backyard. Did I know anything about being a mason and building a wall? Nope. I asked my neighbor, Doug, who was one of my favorite SMEs, to give me an overview. He dropped off a trowel and showed me how to mix cement. I had the attitude of "It couldn't take a mental giant" and confidently launched into building a short wall for my garden.

Doug stopped by a bit later to inspect my wall and entertain himself. "Where's your level line?"

"My what?" I said.

"The line you are following to keep your brick wall straight."

After a blank look from me, he grabbed a piece of kite string and two bricks. He tied the string to the first brick and put it next to the beginning of my wall, then walked to where I had chalked the wall's end and put the other brick with the string tight.

"That's your level line. To make a straight wall, you need to place your bricks against the tight string." Duh, I think!

Parenting is like this. Before you become a parent, you think, "It couldn't take a mental giant," but once the short people show up, you realize the importance of a Doug, your parents, a village, the MOB, books, videos, and professionals. All stages of parenting can be hysterical and terrifying. I learned early that what works for Earnest may not for Exuberance.

Please understand that I am not suggesting that your parenting style matches mine. I share these stories so you know you're not alone, and maybe you will find a tip that will work for your family.

Proof of Life Funds

The man-cubs started testing their limits and pulling away in high school. Exuberance was particularly surly and became hard to live with as he marched toward independence. As I commiserated with another member of the MOB, she stated, "There's a reason caveboys were kicked out of the cave to live on their own as teenagers!" Exuberance was so crazy and mean just before we dropped him off at college that Hon and I literally high-fived each other and shouted, "He's all yours, Sammy!" as we drove out of the university parking lot. Sammy the Seagull was the school mascot.

Exuberance jumped into college with both feet and was determined to have the time of his life. Since he entered college with twelve credits from the community college during his senior year of high school, an aggressively friendly soul and a good judge of a loophole, he realized that he could be the youngest person in the history of the university to join a fraternity. Oh, joy!

In contrast to my sisters-in-law and many friends with girls, it was incredibly difficult to have any regular communication with the boys in college. Earnest was better at answering the phone and texting, but Exuberance was just missing in action too much for my comfort level.

Exuberance and I had a conversation about my issue with his lack of communication. I told him that he needed to talk with me on the phone once a week and that I was willing to pay for it. We negotiated a price of $55 a week and the ground rules for what we called the "proof of life" conversation, in texting shorthand POL$. There were some conditions for the arrangement that needed to occur before I transferred the POL$ into his bank account. He needed to call me; if I called him, it didn't count. We had to have a real conversation, which I qualified as three things: "You need to tell me the best that happened to you that week. You have to tell me the worst thing that happened to you that week, *and* you have to ask me how I am doing."

The best and worst requirement was just a grown-up edition of the high/low game we played during dinner when they were younger. The new piece, asking me how I was doing, was a critical piece of his maturity, as it forced him to think about someone else.

I have talked with friends who are shocked that I paid him to call me once a week. I needed to know how he was doing and was willing to do what I had to in order to keep in touch. The POL$ was only needed for one or two semesters. He got a job on campus as part of the groundskeeping team and loved his access to a golf cart. He was a big man on campus, for sure. Now that he was in the routine of calling us, there was no need to continue to pay him. Our parent/child dynamic began to shift to adult conversations, and a *remarkable transformation* was on the horizon.

The Summer of Shawn

A good friend called one day to see if we'd be willing to house her daughter, Shawn, for the summer, so she could do an internship in DC. She was Earnest's age and heading into her senior year of college. "Of course," I said and ran off to tell Hon the news. We had our house on the market, the revolving door was in full motion as Earnest was heading back to Pennsylvania to find a full-time job, and Exuberance was home from his freshman year of college. Why not add a new family member to the chaos?

Shawn, an only child, did not understand the joy of living with a little brother. No one needed to experience a sister's love and wrath more than Exuberance, who was home for the summer and working as a barback at a popular restaurant. Really, how different could it be having a daughter in the house? Ha!

Shawn and her mom showed up with a car full of clothes, shoes, and makeup. Holy cow! I wasn't sure Earnest's recently abandoned closet was ready for the wardrobe upgrade. Exuberance was not quite sure what to make of the explosion of beauty products in the bathroom he soon shared with Shawn. We all settled into a new routine, each working during the day, and returning to the house in the evening.

Although Hon grew up with five sisters, he was also impressed. "Shawn goes into the bathroom as one person and comes out another. And she wants to talk with me! The boys never want to tell me about their day. It's like pulling teeth, but she wants to tell me all about it. I like this daughter thing."

I was also confused about the daughter communication thing. She would text me throughout the day and call me when she was heading home. It was weird and refreshing. It was also lovely to equalize the testosterone in our house.

Shawn was bewildered by Exuberance, her new bouncy brother, and the sparring that occurred over the bathroom was hysterical. "Exuberance, you can't just walk into my room or the bathroom," Shawn would exclaim. "You have to knock! It's just not cool. And are you using my razor?"

That summer, Earnest returned home for a beach vacation. It was really fun to have the full band together. We managed to sell our house and move to a smaller house that fall. At the end of the year, I sent out a postcard with our new address, which included Shawn in the family picture. Somehow, I managed not to replace the sample name of Bakers in the postcard's template, and the cards arrived, saying, "Happy New Year from The Bakers," not "The Sundius Family." Oops. I sent them out anyway to see who would notice.

The first call I got was from Shawn, who was mad and laughing. "How could you use that photo? I look horrible! And who are the Bakers?" It turns out photos are more important to daughters than sons. Live and learn. Exuberance and Shawn still talk regularly. She became a valuable sounding board for him, offering the female perspective and coaching him on how to be an acceptable boyfriend. Hon and I still love keeping up with our adopted daughter too.

New Year's postcard including Shawn sent out
with the wrong last name printed on it.

The Remarkable Transformation

I call this young adult phase the remarkable transformation because I was happily shocked when it happened. There were many moments when I thought that the boys would never grow up. The back and forth between immaturity and acting like an adult made my head spin. And then, suddenly, I realized they *got it*! It was truly remarkable when they transformed into functioning adults.

As typical of my parenting experience, their transformations were different in action and timing. In general, it was sometime in their early twenties, and it was one of the most rewarding realizations of my life.

Empty Nest

Empty nest is such a silly name. If you've done your MOB job well, your family will always come home to visit, so your nest is never really empty. Good grief! Hon and I decided to get our house ready to be put on the market and downsize after Exuberance left for college. We needed to reduce our overhead, so we could help pay for college. It took us nine months of renovating, painting, and purging junk to get the house ready to put on the market. The weekend of our first open house, Earnest came home after completing his junior year at college. The three of us decided to go to the beach and recover from renovating and college. Since the boys were living their lives and heading in different directions, it was fun when we had the opportunity to enjoy one-on-one time with them.

Over that weekend, Hon and I asked Earnest to pull up his second-semester grades. He had been struggling with a class, and we hadn't been paying as close attention since we were focused on renovating the house. During his sophomore year, Earnest switched majors from engineering to computer science and cybersecurity. The university required all students of that major to take the computer programming language COBOL. Reluctantly, he logged into the portal and looked up his grade.

"I got a D again," he admitted. He had taken that course in the first semester too. "The major requires that I get at least a C. There's only one professor that teaches this class."

Hon jumps in. "COBOL? Are you taking COBOL? Why? I took COBOL when I was in college. It's a very old programming language. I thought it was dead."

"The school says it's still being used by government agencies and the banking system, and there are not enough programmers. They think it's important for us to understand."

Hon rolled his eyes with concern. "Why don't you transfer to a Maryland school? Cybersecurity is a big initiative in our state. Your school is not equipped to take on this major."

"I've already signed my lease for an apartment with my friends. We just moved our stuff into it. I was really looking forward to living with them," said Earnest.

We continued the conversation with thoughtfulness and calm throughout the weekend. After discussing a few options with Earnest, he decided to pause his college experience. We all agreed that his current school was not the best match for his chosen career in IT and cybersecurity, and it didn't make sense to continue to pay for an expensive education that wasn't working for him. Hon and I knew that he had found his tribe of great friends, and we wanted to help him reach a decision that supported his path to independence.

In the end, Earnest decided to go back and find a full-time job, so he could support himself and continue to live with his buddies. Allowing him to make the decision that was right for him and encouraging his chosen path was a big step in his confidence and in our understanding of how to parent a young adult. Earnest got a job as a contractor at an IT help desk and worked there for three years, completely self-sufficient and off our payroll.

This three-year period was a remarkable transformation for Earnest. As a family, we supported his decision and even visited him with food, dishes, and pots and pans to cook a Thanksgiving dinner in his bachelor pad because he was unable to get off work. He moved home at the beginning of COVID-19, then at age twenty-three, he was a confident, happy young man.

He worked at a new help desk job with a large investment firm and set himself up in our basement for a year during COVID-19. The three of us worked out from our downsized house, enjoying each other. That year was a gift in many ways, full of homemade sourdough bread and puzzles. Hon and I were blown away at how good he was on the phone and nicknamed him the grandpa whisperer, as he repeatedly guided elderly callers on how to reset their passwords.

"No, don't restart the computer, just the browser. That's all right. I'll wait for your computer to come back online," would drift up through the basement floor from Earnest as he coached callers. The struggle was real when explaining directions for how to use two-factor authentication. He is the most patient person I know.

I share this story of Earnest pausing college because it was tricky to navigate as a parent. Hon and I learned and accepted that it was our job to support our boy's path forward. Earnest was able to save a lot of money because he joined the job market early and put his income in the bank during COVID-19. His hard work and savings allowed him to be able to buy a small townhouse at the age of twenty-five. He also transferred his college credits to a university in Maryland and should graduate in cybersecurity when he's about twenty-seven. This will be a huge accomplishment, given that he has been working full-time, finishing his degree online, and paying for this final part of his education since we paid for the first three years.

There are more options today for a successful career and life than there were when Hon and I were growing up. We realized during that moment at the beach that it was our job to support Earnest's path forward, not dictate it. Today, he is a successful, independent adult and has built a future that is just right for him.

Credit Cards and Responsibility

Financial literacy is barely taught in school, which is unfortunate. We did our best with our highly mediocre parenting strategy of making the boys work to earn their own money, but managing a bank account does not translate to credit card management.

Exuberance, always in a hurry to do everything, signed up to get one of those special credit cards designed to entice college students with no money. Since he was a legal adult, he didn't need our permission to get it, and proudly explained that it would help him grow his credit. In my opinion, it's abusive to naive poor students, and he was a sucker.

The summer between his sophomore and junior years, Exuberance got himself a job at a large seafood restaurant at the beach and lived in his apartment near school since he rented year-round off campus. He attacked being a waiter with his usual gusto, and Hon and I were amused that he was keeping a spreadsheet to track his upsells and tips. Really! Is there anything you don't want to top with crab imperial for an additional twenty dollars?

"The cute blonde waitresses typically get higher tips than me," explained Exuberance. "But I beat them on Sunday brunch. The grandmas love me!"

Exuberance, continuing to live his best life, learned several valuable lessons that summer. One lesson was that in the eyes of a popular seasonal restaurant, he was just a cog. We eventually realized he was tracking his tips because he thought the restaurant was skimming off the top. It turns out they were. He was angry at the way he was being treated and, unbeknown to us, quit the job well before college started up again and had a fabulous, fun summer.

As his savings ran out, he turned to his credit card to get by. In his mind, he'd be able to pay it off with his groundskeeping job when school started up again. He called shortly into that fall semester to confess that he had left the summer job early and run up his credit card.

Hon and I went to visit him that weekend to come up with a solution. We discussed the predatory nature of the credit card he had with an interest rate of over 20 percent. Hon and I appreciated the stress of being financially overcommitted and explained that it's why we recently downsized to live within our means. He was tackling a valuable life lesson early.

Hon and I did not want to pay off his credit card, which had a balance under $1,500. We thought it was important for him to take care of his own debt.

"How about this, Exuberance," I said. "I will transfer money into your bank account monthly, so you may pay the minimum due, but it will be your responsibility to remind me each month and keep us informed about the balance. It will also be your responsibility to fully pay off your credit card. I am just giving you the minimum to protect your future credit."

He accepted his responsibility and didn't need my help paying off the credit card a few months later after increasing his hours working on campus. The remarkable transformation really kicked in that year as he learned to balance work, fun, and finances. Having a girlfriend really sped the remarkable transformation process along too, as they can grow weary of the shenanigans.

When the boys turned twenty-one, Hon and I gave them a book that we had read, *The Wealthy Barber: Everyone's Commonsense Guide to Becoming Financially Independent* by David Chilton. It explained the basics of managing personal finances in an easy-to-read story about tips from the town barber who was very wealthy. Both boys appreciated learning about compound interest in a 401k plan, the advantage of a Roth IRA, and the importance of a 10 percent fund. Its guidance enabled Earnest to be able to buy his townhouse when he was twenty-five. Teaching your children financial literacy is not easy, and the Wealthy Barber helped fill in the gaps for the boys.

Internships

Internships and experience with different careers were crucial to the path of independence. I have already told you about Earnest's experience, coding with his uncle when he was in high school. He also interned with my brother, organizing files and creating PowerPoint presentations. We leaned on friends for jobs for the boys too.

One summer, Earnest worked as a production assistant for a friend, Mike, who installed television studios. Mike nicknamed Earnest, The Terminator, after he perfected cutting video cables and adding the appropriate connection to the end.

Mike called Earnest one morning, "Where are you? You're late." Earnest proclaimed sleepily, "But I texted you to ask if we were working today, and you texted back, '10–4.' It's only 8:30."

There was a heavy sigh on the other end, as Mike realized he had jumped the generation gap, and trucker CB radio shorthand was probably not the best way to communicate to Gen Z. "My bad," he said. "Just hustle over here." We still laugh about that one.

Exuberance also had the gift of an incredible internship. His internship plans between his junior and senior years of college had been canceled due to COVID-19. He needed a positive work experience for his resume and mental health. One of his cousin's husbands offered to hire him to work with him in a large chain of BBQ equipment stores in Houston, Texas, and off he went.

Exuberance had been driving a manual Toyota Matrix with many miles on it for a few years. Marge the Matrix was a perfect car for him, as it kept him fully engaged in driving with all four limbs moving in tandem. We got Marge a tune-up, and Exuberance and his girlfriend headed south, staying with cousins in Atlanta and New Orleans on their way to Texas.

His girlfriend headed home on a plane, and as with all things, he jumped into this new experience with both feet. Exuberance was staying with his cousin, Abby, and her husband, Jared, who were both in their early thirties. He was going to have to play up, pretending to be much older than his twenty-two years. Abby grew up with three sisters and experienced a similar shock to Shawn's at living with a bouncy young male cousin. I advised her that he was not a sister and would not read between the lines. If something he was doing bothered her, she would just have to explain it plainly. Jared embraced his role of mentor to his new protégé.

Exuberance's first week of work was Memorial Day weekend, and the local television station was reporting live from the BBQ store during the morning show. Jared put Exuberance on camera, and he pitched the advantages of a grill that he had learned about the night before. The lessons learned that summer are numerous. Jared and Abby opened their home and hearts, shared their friends and family, and were a pivotal accelerant to the remarkable transformation. One of the incredible tips Exuberance learned was to dress for success on your last day of work. He put on the only suit he had, shook everyone's hand, and thanked them for the experience. Suits were not the typical work attire at the BBQ store.

At the end of the summer, I took time off work and flew to Texas to drive home with Exuberance in Marge the Matrix. We took advantage of the drive and our love of music. Marge puttered along through Texas and Arkansas, stopping in Memphis, Tennessee. Exuberance was all about Nashville, but I explained that Memphis was on my bucket list. Since I was funding this exploration, we were going to spend two nights in Memphis and one in Nashville. After visiting Beale Street and experiencing ribs and blues, he appreciated my wisdom. We also visited Graceland and all that was Elvis, but the highlight for both of us was the Sun Studio. Sun is a recording studio and the birthplace of rock 'n' roll in my mind, and we listened to playlists of music recorded there all the way back to Maryland. I will forever cherish that trip and the time I was able to spend with Jared, Abby, and Exuberance.

It is a gift to be able to go on a trip with your young adult child. For me, it helped me appreciate and respect the young man he had become. The drive alone was over twenty-two hours. We listened to music and podcasts, called various cousins of Exuberance, shared stories, and had heart-to-heart conversations. Our relationship was forever changed for the better during that trip, and we got to show off our cool Texas cowboy and cowgirl wear.

Suzy and Exuberance exploring Nashville on the drive home from Texas.

Winning the Lottery

Exuberance got a job in digital marketing shortly after graduating college and made Sammy the Seagull (his school's mascot) and us proud. With both boys off the payroll, Hon and I felt like we had won the lottery. We still have some educational loans to pay off, but we see a future of maybe being debt-free. A girl can dream, right? The boys charted their own paths, and we learned to support, not lead them.

The transformation that I experienced in my twenties was significant. Who I was at twenty was a remarkably different person than who I was at thirty. I have shared those lessons with my children and my nieces and nephews.

I believe in your twenties, you need to have your heart broken, so you appreciate love. You need to live on the brink of poverty, so you empathize with those less fortunate than you. And you need to be taken advantage of by an employer, so you value and recognize a good boss and workplace. It is easier to check those boxes while you are young and single. Once you have a life partner and children and assets, those lessons are much harder to learn. I encourage the boys to take advantage of this stage in their life. There's no need to rush. The best things in life are worth waiting for and getting right.

> **Tip: Life Steps for Twenty-Somethings**
>
> A professor I worked for during college offered these basic life steps, which I have relayed to my boys and anyone who will listen.
>
> First, you get a plant.
> If the plant lives, you can get a pet.
> If the pet lives, you can get a spouse.
> If the marriage is successful, you can have children.
> Don't do it out of order!

Fly Gen Z Fly

So here we are at the end of this book. I've shared our triumphs and challenges and offered many survival tips. There are no guarantees that my tips will work with your children, but I encourage you to embrace all the stages and share your journey with your tribe.

This is not the end of my story either. I continue to learn how to be a better mother. The boys are now several years into their careers. Serious girlfriends are now part of the equation, and I do my best to be kind and supportive and not interfere in their relationships. I know from my own experience that affairs of the heart can be complicated, and the head and the heart don't always agree. I've learned over the years that a girlfriend one day, may not be the one the next, and I may never know why. It's OK; it's not my business. I try to listen and not comment too much, for you never know when the off relationship might turn on again.

Of course, my life is all wrapped up in a bow now. Ha! That's super funny. I'm still a juggler, helping my parents, who are both in their eighties, and the boys, and working to put money away for retirement. I still struggle with life balance, but I am better at it than I used to be. There are many adventures to come: weddings, grandchildren, retirement, and new life chapters. Live and learn, right?

It is also my hope that by sharing my journey of motherhood, the good times and the bad, it will help you, dear members of the MOB, and that we can encourage the next generation to exceed the last.

Exuberance and Earnest fully adulting in their twenties.

About the Author

I am the oldest of two children. My brother, twenty-one months younger, was always strong and competitive. He toughened me up for sure! My mother was a kindergarten teacher, and my father was a salesman and entrepreneur.

I graduated from Kutztown University of Pennsylvania with a BS in television production and have always loved my ever-evolving career in communications and storytelling. Hon and I married in our early thirties and were blessed to have two boys, whom I call Earnest and Exuberance in this book.

I am sharing our adventures in parenthood because I feel that our current culture tends to exaggerate, hide, and sugarcoat the challenges parents face in raising kids to be responsible adults. Hon and I learned not to be overly reactive and to try to understand the situation before jumping to conclusions. Parenting is the hardest job on earth.

Since I am not an expert on parenting or child rearing, I am launching a companion podcast to the book, also called *The Mothers of Boys Survival Guide*. The podcast will be specifically for mothers of boys, and experts and other members of the MOB will be invited to discuss a variety of topics. Since moms don't have much free time, the podcasts will be short. I hope you join the MOB and help continue this critical topic. Please visit the mothersofboys.life website to join the conversation and learn more.